STRANGE CASES
AND
WILD TALES

Lewis M. Ress

First published in the United States of America in 2018

ISBN: 9781798950418

Dedication

I asked my editor and publisher, Chris Fagg, of London, England, who just happens to be married to my wife's niece, how to create an unusual dedication. Actually, there aren't many, if any, unique dedications. He said: "The book started as a dinner conversation in, of all places, Iceland...". That's pretty unusual. I started to tell some pretty wild, but true, stories. Chris encouraged me to share them. My niece, Ellin Stein, who is a famous author in her own right, said that I could write a book.

My wife, Esta Berkall, said that I should take a chance. How could I ignore her? She took the biggest chance of her life when she married me.

This book is dedicated to Chris Fagg, Ellin Stein and my wife.

Contents

1

Round One

Angelo Dundee was the trainer of Muhammad Ali and he gave me a boxing lesson.

"Punch with your left fist... Say 'One' to yourself. Then punch with your right fist and say 'Three' to yourself. Fast! One... Three! One... Three!"

"Angelo, what happens with 'Two'?"

"That's when he hits you."

The first part of this trip winds up like many adventures, at the shore of a remote barrier island... Miami Beach. I realized that my father wasn't a God despite what Mr. Ullizzi might have believed. I wasn't a superlawyer, and although I probably in some ways did a little better than my father and my sons probably did better than I, my grandsons could wind up back in my grandparents' coffee and tea business, starting the cycle all over.

Arthur Godfrey may have been a virulent anti-Semite. I suggest that you ask around. His hotel, The Blue Waters, was alleged to display a sign: "No dogs or Jews."

But he strummed his ukulele on the radio and publicized Miami Beach in the early days. So they named a major crossroad for him at 41st Street. It's "Arthur Godfrey Road." Try walking down that street nowadays. Groups of bearded men are there all in black with wide-brimmed hats. The women are walking behind with long black dresses, long sleeves and scarves on their heads. They are walking to the synagogue. The restaurants only serve kosher food. The Orthodox Jews have taken over Arthur Godfrey Road and Arthur Godfrey must be rolling over in his grave.

There's the bell. The end of Round One.

2

Mr. Ullizzi

My father was the only one in his large family that went to college. And no one else in the family was a "professional man." They came from Lithuania and were for the most part in the coffee and tea business. He went to Brooklyn Law School and ate one-cent sandwiches and struggled. One-cent sandwiches were two pieces of white bread with nothing in between. Two-cent sandwiches had a piece of baloney in the middle.

My dad had a small law office on Court Street in Brooklyn, just room for his chair, a small desk and two client chairs. He shared a reception room with another lawyer as well as his secretary, who was his sister, Berdie. He used to come home and tell us stories at dinner. One of the best was how he was sitting at his desk early one morning when a client rushed in wearing only pajamas and slippers. He was quite agitated, shaking from head to toe. He kept shouting "Mr. Ress, I love you. Mr. Ress, I love you!"

He dropped to his knees in front of the desk and said:

"Mr. Ress, You' a my God! You'a my God! You save'a my life! You save'a my life!"

"Mr. Ullizzi, take it easy. Are you alright? What happened?"

Mr. Ullizzi remains on his knees and looks up at my father with widened eyes. He is shaking. His hands are clasped over his chest.

"Mr. Ress I was in Long Island, in my car, driving. I was coming up to the Long Island Railroad crossing. I look'a to the left. I look'a to the right. I start across the tracks. She's'a all clear. And then I see this big a black train. She's a coming down on me fast. I know I'm'a gonna die. So I say: 'Mr. Ress, my attorney, what do I do?'

And you answer me!

'*Mr. Ullizzi, throw yourself on the floor of the car, throw yourself on the floor!*'

So I always follow your advice and I throw myself on the floor. The train, she comes like lightning and smashes my car. Everything goes black. I wake up in the hospital, but I'm'a OK. They won't let me out. I have to stay under observation. I say to myself that I must go to Mr. Ress and thank him. So I get out of bed and climb out the window. There is a fire escape and I go down to the street and I take a taxi to you.

Thank you. Thank you Mr. Ress

Mr. Ress, you save'a my life.

You'a my God!"

I was hooked.

3

Travel

"Only in America!"

"Son, there are two ways of making a success in the practice of law. One way is to enjoy your education. Have fun. Join a fraternity. Party. Meet the daughter of the senior partner in a prestigious law firm and marry her. The other way is to study very hard and be extremely competitive. Be a leader. Get into an Ivy League law school. Be at the top of your class. Make Law Review. Get a job at the best law firm in town. Come in early. Work late. Grind it out on weekends and holidays. Write briefs that the supervising partner will take credit for... and after three years marry the boss's daughter." My father believed the truth in that joke.

I literally believed that America was the land of opportunity and that no matter where you came from if you gave it your best and were honest, good things would happen to you and you would share in the American dream and could be a big success, That was the American way. I was a true believer.

Move to Florida, the land of opportunity. Southern Hospitality. Mint juleps. Pecan pie. Magnolia trees. Sippin' bourbon.

Gentlemanly manners. Hold the door open for the ladies. Men dress in white suits. Soft speech, a sort of drawl. Fried catfish and hush puppies. Warm nights with heavy moist air and the scent of gardenias.

Not exactly.

*   *   *   *   *

It was hot as hell in June 1956, and my wife and I had packed our few belongings, left New York and headed down US1 to Florida to start a new life. We had her car, a '54 Chevy with no air conditioning and it was well over ninety degrees every day. You couldn't put your arm out of the open window while you were driving. It was that hot. We pulled up at nine-dollar-a-night roadside motels with neon signs, where you park at the door to your room. We ate at burger stands. This was our honeymoon, but we were on our own and optimistic.

Crossing the Florida State Line we talked about where to live—anyplace but Miami. I started calling law firms around the state to which I had written. It was premature. The Florida Bar exam was coming up soon and I hadn't even taken a preparation course

My résumé looked pretty good. Anyhow I thought so. Cornell Law School. Admitted to the New York Bar. Two years as a Contracting Officer in the Army Ordnance Corps, stationed on Wall Street with the elite Top Secret military-civilian team contracting for highly sensitive anti-missile missiles, spending over a billion dollars of the Army's money. There should be no problem getting a position with a "prestigious" law firm. Boy, was I wrong!

6

Driving down the east coast of Florida it became clear that there was little or no industry and that the sluggish economy was primarily dependent on tourism. There was no need for Ivy League, Yankee lawyers.

Miami was the only city with some life, some business buzz, some future potential, especially with trade to South America through Miami increasing…. Still, there was little possibility for a job. Cornell Law School was the key to opening doors for a number of interviews with substantial Miami firms. Blackwell, Walker and Gray; Shutts and Bowen; Nichols, Gaither, Green…. and more. Their offices were each furnished in "early bank" with heavy drapes, thick carpets, dark mahogany furniture and brass lamps. The walls were lined with gold-framed oil paintings, portraits of the founding partners. The lawyers wore dark suits, white shirts, striped ties, black shoes and close-cropped haircuts with no facial hair. Mostly they had graduated from the University of Florida Law School and had attended Southern colleges maybe going as far north as The Citadel. They were all white, southern, Christian men. Not one woman! No Northerners! No Jews! (Blacks? Hispanics?—You're kidding! Forget it.)

The nicer ones were frank.

"Lewis, we really like you and you would fit right in, but one of our partners…. you know…. He won't have any Jews in the firm."

"Lewis, you are so very well qualified, but we really think that you would be happier in New York."

"Almost all of the Jewish lawyers are over on Miami Beach. You should look there."

The time to take the Bar exam was approaching. It was only

given in Tallahassee and took three days of writing eight essays per day. We drove north on Route 27. The air was so thick with humidity you could cut it with a knife. The Florida cities and towns were slow-moving places built up around town squares with green lawns, large shade trees, benches and almost always a large bronze or granite statue of a Confederate soldier. He would be standing (usually an ordinary soldier) or on horseback (often a general) in the center of the square. The statue was donated by the Daughters of the Confederacy, often draped in Confederate flags, with a list of those who served and those who died in the cause of the Confederacy engraved into the base.

Just across the street there would be the old white-columned courthouse raised up about six steps with a rusted fire escape on the side of the building. There were no malls or chain restaurants. Locals chatted at the coffee shop, just on the edge of the square, with linoleum floors and a menu that also featured catfish and hushpuppies. Orlando was a slow, sleepy place with redbrick streets and one old hotel. Ocala had one restaurant, the Silver Dollar, and all the black population was confined to a ghetto type slum area. (It still is.)

The further north we drove, the more Southern the area became. Tallahassee was typical. Old two-story plantation homesteads for the rich, and wooden shacks with outhouses for the poor. The main activity was politics, mostly conducted at the Silver Slipper restaurant in "private" back rooms, thick with cigar smoke. The government clerks were all white and moved in slow motion. The men wore red suspenders in addition to belts to reassure that their pants wouldn't drop. Everyone spoke with a deep southern accent, but they were always friendly and helpful.

My wife read out loud from a set of Bar preparation notes which was a gift from another New Yorker, who never made it through. One had to know that miscegenation (a racially mixed marriage) was grounds for an annulment. One party had only to be one-eighth black. That was the test ... and the marriage was null and void. Women could do little, if anything without their husband's consent. They were treated like the husband's personal property. Cattle had the right of way over cars. Any amount of a driver's contributory negligence was a bar to recovery in an auto collision. Segregation was everywhere. "Separate but equal" was the law. There was no such thing as "equal." Separate—yes sir. You bet!

Black people lived in slums, wooden-slatted windows, shacks, ghettos. No running water. Galvanized metal tubs hung from the rear door. The Saturday night bath water was heated in kettles and used three or four times. No inside plumbing. Out-houses. Muddy unpaved streets. Blacks couldn't walk on the sidewalk if there were whites on it. They couldn't go into a "white" movie theater, restaurant or into a hotel, much less stay there. Their schools were worse than those in third-world countries. There were poll taxes, and oral and written exams for voting rights. In the mornings black men stood in knots on the street corners looking for day-labor jobs and when a pickup truck stopped, they jumped in the back. The Klan and the "White Citizens' Council" organizations were everywhere. Education, the key to "breaking out", was closed to blacks. They were trapped.

The Bar exam was conducted in a room without air conditioning for three days. My sweat was dripping on the desk. I wrote and wrote. Eight essays each day. At night my wife could not understand why we went to the movies instead of studying. I knew that it was too late! We left for Sarasota, down Florida's west coast and then around Lake Okeechobee on the two-lane roads. Across from the lake and just off the road, there was a rundown wooden shack. A bar with a huge sign on the roof, like a billboard, the size of the entire building. It faced directly to the road. It read:

4

Learn to Play Tennis

I had learned to play tennis as a child, played on my high school team and in my senior year I was a ball boy at Forest Hills and had my picture taken with the finalists, Pancho Gonzales and Ted Schroeder, on the balcony of the West Side Tennis Club. In those days you kept playing until you won the set by two games and in the final set of the match Gonzales defeated Schroeder twenty to eighteen. They wore spikes and the grass court was all chewed up.

The public tennis courts in North Miami Beach were hard polished concrete located behind City Hall. There was an open-air palm thatch roof over the corner of a stone wall at one end of the court area which was the office from which the tennis pro assigned courts and sold tennis balls. His name was Nick Bolletieri and he became the world-famous tennis coach. He introduced me to Bernie Sayer and we played.

"Lewis, what do you do for a living?... If you practice law the way you play tennis, you are a tiger! Would you like to do some legal work for me?"

"I would love to."

"You didn't even ask me what I do."

"I know. I'll do anything."

"I'm an adjuster with the Aetna Casualty and Surety Company. What do you know about 'friendly' suits?"

"Nothing."

"I'll teach you."

By this time the Florida Bar results had come in and I was number two in the state. My boss, George Case, seemed unimpressed, but my salary went up to fifty dollars a week. I still didn't have enough to buy any office furniture. Maybe this would be my big break.

Bernie explained that friendly suits are the legal papers used to settle the claims of children. You have to set out the facts, describe the accident and the injuries, explain the settlement amount, showing that it was in the child's best interests and ask the Judge to approve it. A parent is usually named guardian of the funds. Following Bernie's forms, which came from one of the big downtown law firms, and using the information from his file, it took me about an hour to prepare the papers. Bernie would bring the parents and sometimes the child to the courthouse. We could walk it through the very accommodating Court and come away with an Order Approving Settlement in about another hour. It was short and simple. My first bill came back with a note from Bernie Sayer. "Call me." The conversation was short.

"Double the bill and it will be half of what the big boys charge." That one bill was more than my entire monthly salary!

Bernie sent me two friendly suits a week. I had furniture in the office.

Bernie and I were having nineteen-cent burgers at White Castle.

"What do you know about workers' compensation?"

"Nothing."

That wasn't exactly accurate. I had assisted in one workers' compensation case with George Case for the estate of a deceased ironworker. George had been an ironworker and now represented the Union-Management organization, which conducted educational training and management negotiations. We had won, but I was observing George.

"The Stanley Works" (Stanley Tool Company) has a fractured coccyx case that they are quite concerned about and I would like you to defend it. They are a national assured and they have been unhappy with our not winning a single compensation case for them in the State of Florida."

The initial part of the case involved taking the sworn statement of the employee. This is called a deposition and the employee is called the claimant. We lawyers have created our own language to pretty much cover up how simple most of the law practice really is. The main thing to know about workers' compensation is that it is a rough-and-tumble practice. The Judge, (Deputy Commissioner), listens to the parties and the witnesses, examines the evidence and makes all the findings of fact and decides the damages. It is a one-man band and he rules! There also was a presumption that the injury was related to the employment.

Workers' comp lawyers are not the most elegant, refined, well-mannered gentlemen. All of them were men. It was a scramble with objections flying all over the place. That is exactly what happened during my first deposition. The claimant's lawyer continually shouted objections.

"Objection! It's leading! Don't answer that question. It's already been asked and answered and my client said that her back hit the table on the way down to the floor. Tell him how you hurt your back against that table."

I went over to the Stanley Window plant, which was not far from our office. It was huge, noisy, with dust in the air. They showed me the large table against which the claimant, Yolanda Byron, said she had struck her back. Something didn't feel right. There were two fellow workers who witnessed the fall and confirmed the immediate onset of pain. The ambulance records had the same history of striking her back against the table as she fell to the floor, as did the hospital records, which I obtained by subpoena. The x-rays clearly showed a fractured coccyx. I took her doctor's deposition. Based on her history he related the fracture to the accident and he found that she suffered a fifteen percent permanent disability to the body as a whole and could not engage in lifting over fifteen pounds. Plus, no repetitive bending, and no standing on her feet for over one hour at a time in a work environment. He swore that Yolanda would need periodic therapy for the remainder of her life. The claimant's employment expert stated that with her limited education and her physical restrictions and ongoing pain keeping her from being able to concentrate, Yolanda was unemployable in the open labor market. Yolanda Byron was thirty-one years old and had a long work life expectancy. He stated that she might ultimately need attendant care. I noted that the doctor never said that.

The Stanley people were really upset. Lifetime medical benefits came to very big numbers, like over one million dollars. In addition worker's comp benefits for Yolanda's lifetime, reduced to present worth value, was also a huge sum. On top of it all, if they lost they were responsible for the Yolanda's attorneys' fees and all of the expert witness fees and costs. We're talking in the millions.

I spoke to a conservative orthopedic surgeon who questioned the history.

"Almost all fractured coccyx come from a sitting-down compression injury when one hits the hard ground, with the trauma coming directly to the base of the spine, not from a glancing blow like striking an object on the way down."

Yet her medical history appeared to be clean. Yolanda Byron had moved to Miami about a year ago from Houston, Texas. Her employment application showed no past low-back or spinal injuries. She passed the pre-employment physical. She had worked hard and regularly up until the day of the accident, with no lost time. Her work evaluations were good. Her employment application showed her social security number and her past address in Houston.

I don't know what motivated me, but her case was too perfect. Something seemed wrong. I subpoenaed any records relating to her from all five hospitals in Houston, setting out her social security number and prior address. At that time we were allowed to send out investigative subpoenas without filing with the Deputy Commissioner or giving any notice to the other side.

BINGO!

At Houston General Hospital a little over one year earlier there was a record of a fractured coccyx, from hitting the floor. Same lady: Yolanda Byron!

The Final Hearing went forward before a grouchy Deputy

Commissioner. The witnesses confirmed Yolanda's tearful story. Since the accident she couldn't bend over, couldn't drive a car, had to be helped with the groceries, required rest periods in bed. The doctor swore that she was fifteen percent disabled and listed her permanent limitations and her need for ongoing medical care. Their employment expert testified at length, describing all of the tests he performed and declared her to be "unemployable." The Deputy Commissioner was about to rule against us. (The benefits for life came to over three million dollars.)

"Your Honor, I have one witness only, who is listed third from the bottom on my witness list. I call the custodian of the records of Houston General Hospital."

It took less than five minutes. The Deputy Commissioner slammed his gavel on the desk. The sound was like an explosion. I jumped.

"GET HER OUT OF HERE!" shouted the Commissioner.

"CLAIM DENIED!"

After that Stanley wanted me to handle all of their cases in South Florida and the Aetna made me their workers' compensation specialist.

It's good that I learned to play tennis.

5

Meet the Boss

The Aetna Casualty was known as the "Cadillac" of insurance companies. Those were the days of the "Fleetwood" and the "El Dorado" with chrome strips along the sides and huge rear fins. Cadillac was synonymous with "prestige" and "the best." To be an Aetna attorney was a Cadillac pedigree. You were respected. You actually represented their insured clients and some of them were very, very prestigious, including Stanley Tool Company, Chrysler Corporation, The Catholic Diocese, Walgreens, The University of Miami and the local CBS Television Channel. It opened doors.

The Aetna had its claims offices on West Flagler Street near Northwest 27th Avenue, on the ground floor. I went down there to meet the claims manager. Mr. Ivey, the Southeast Claims Manager, was an older, humorless, balding man with a narrow face and a thin narrow tie dangling inside an ill-fitting light tan sports coat. Evidently he was a "yankee", but had acclimated and adapted to the South. Mr. Ivey didn't say very much. He told me that he wanted me to meet Mr. Benton, just across the hall. I looked for my tennis friend, Bernie, a claims adjuster, who had a desk along with ten other Aetna adjusters in somewhat cramped quarters. He was not there. Bernie had been a true mentor. He was not happy having to deal with the imperious attorneys at the larger downtown firms. He found them arrogant and overpriced and above all prejudiced. That was why he sponsored me and guided me. He was trying to dislodge them

At Bernie's suggestion I had gone out with him and his photographer, Sal, at the inception of certain large cases in order to gain better perspective, meet with the witnesses and examine the accident scene—and it worked. It provided valuable insight into the case and even more importantly it pleased Bernie. Bernie had recommended me to his fellow adjusters once I was on the "approved" list. The business was rolling in, both in workers' compensation and automobile liability. It was now time to meet the real boss, but Bernie was not there to introduce and support me. I felt like a lamb being led to the slaughter.

The Aetna office was in the same building owned by a big insurance agency, Benton, Jefferson and Smith. They were right across the hall from the Aetna. The building was named the "Benton Building" and there was a large sign on the roof:

"Benton, Jefferson & Smith Insurance Agency"
"Aetna Casualty And Surety Company"

Although the Benton insurance agency placed insurance with many insurance companies, the Aetna was special. The relationship was close, with friends in the main state office in Tampa and relatives in the Aetna's home office in Hartford. The Benton yacht was always available when executives came down from Connecticut in February. The Benton group were University of Miami graduates and trustees and they placed the

18

insurance for the "U" with the Aetna. They all drove Cadillacs, had fifty-yard line football tickets and memberships in the Bath, Surf and other "restricted" clubs where they entertained frequently. These were rich, powerful people.

Mr. Ivcy took me across the hall to introduce me to the Benton group. The three partners had large glass-enclosed private offices with high-backed executive chairs. Each office was decorated with University of Miami memorabilia, certificates of awards of all types, bronze statues, medals, plaques, footballs, banners and pictures with the university's past and present presidents. There were about fifty agents working at their own grey metal desks, all lined up in three rows in front of the partners' offices. We were heading toward the conference room and I could see three large men in suits with vests already seated at the table. There wasn't a Jew or a black or a Hispanic in sight. I had the distinct feeling that I was being produced and displayed and examined for Benton's approval. Mr. Benton, Senior, was a known anti-Semite. That "uncomfortable" feeling was coming over me.

Just then one of the junior executives came rushing out of the conference room and exclaimed: "Hey, you're Lew Ress, from George Case's office. I know you. I'm Steve Christie and George and I are in Kiwanis together."

He took me by the arm and escorted me into the conference room.

"Gentlemen, this is Lew Ress, George Case's associate, and he's a great guy."

I guess Steve Christie saved the day for me. I was accepted.

19

6

It was 1960

It was 1960. The Aetna had a new claims manager. He arrived from Hartford and had never been in Florida before. His name was Bill Connors. The Aetna claims office was now located on the top floor, the entire top floor, of a Coral Gables high-rise office building at 95 Merrick Way. The office space was large, all decorated in muted green; light-green metal desks, moss-green leather chairs, sea-green file cabinets and thick carpeting, all soft green, with over fifty claims adjusters and supervisors plus safety engineers, accountants, secretaries, file clerks and two receptionists. They were now my biggest client, but I always felt uncomfortable. With all of the people, the bustle, the hum of business being done, it was clear to me that there was a total absence of blacks, Hispanics, Jews and women in non-menial jobs. Not a single one.

Bill Connors looked like a Bill Connors. He had white, white skin, Irish eyes and a pug nose. He wore a dark-brown suit, with brown wing-tipped shoes and would you believe a green tie? His hair was getting white and thinning and you could hear the New England twang in his voice. He was a "by the book" company man.

"Mr. Ress, sit down it's about time we met."

"Mr. Connors, it's a pleasure to meet you, sir. I want you to know that I am proud to represent the Aetna Casualty and Surety Company"… and so the conversation went. One thing led to another and finally I said, "but I don't know if you will feel comfortable having me as one of your attorneys. You see I'm Jewish. I believe that the Aetna doesn't have a single Jewish employee or use a Jewish attorney anywhere in the entire State of Florida. I would understand it if you preferred that I didn't represent you."

"Lewis, you raise a very significant question. Let me think about it and I'll get back to you."

I figured "that was it!" and my biggest client, the one that supported our entire office was going to be "gone." My friend Bernie was back at the home office in Hartford. He could do nothing for me and I had been on my own at the Aetna for over a year. Life is not always fair.

After two weeks of fretting I got the call.

"Mr. Connors would like to see you in his office, as soon as is convenient."

I was there in two hours.

Mr. Connors was sitting in his large glass enclosed office at the head of the lines of desks, sipping coffee.

"Sit down Mr. Ress, I want you to meet two of our newest adjusters, Mel Kornblum and Samuel Cohen."

With that two men entered the room and shook hands. I don't believe in stereotypes, but boy, were they Jewish! There was no mistaking it. They were clearly Jewish.

After they left, he said:

"Lewis, do they look Jewish enough? I made it a point to hire so that there will be no doubt as to where we stand. This is the start. I promise you that we will have blacks, Hispanics, and women."

"Mr. Connors, you have made a friend for life."

And it was true. And it was to be.

*   *   *   *   *

Sequel:

Many, many years, later Bill Connors was sitting at his desk when a call came in from the Tampa state office. He had a run-in with the State manager. Bill insisted that the Company rulebook was very specific about a certain item. The State manager said,

"I don't give a damn about the book, do what I tell you."

Bill said:

"I work for the Aetna, not for you."

One week later he got a call. "Pack up your gear and be out of the office within five minutes. You are fired."

Bill Connors, the Company man, who probably put the Company ahead of everything and everybody in his life except his wife, was OUT! And after twenty-five years of loyalty he was NOBODY.

It's amazing what happens when you don't have power any more. Bill worked as a claims supervisor for a large taxi company. Then, no job. He went downhill fast. Where were all the attorneys who he had helped make wonderful fees? Only one showed up regularly to visit to take him out to dinner and to care. Where were all the "good times" people who had wined and dined him when he could send them business? Gone. My wife and I continued to take Bill and his wife out to dinner.

Bill retreated into a corner of his den, which was a dark room, and he didn't want to come out. Esta brought her brisket (boiled beef), which he loved. Bill hated onions; even the word "onion" got him upset. My wife's brisket was loaded with onions. What Bill didn't know didn't hurt him. He was crazy over her brisket. However, Bill didn't last too long. He just rapidly mentally degenerated and died.

Who looked in on his widow and told her what a great man he was?

She already knew.

7

Hand-to-Hand Combat

John Mathews' life was a mess. He was single, bitter, angry and frustrated. He was clenching his teeth. The veins on the side of his head were bulging. Here he was back in the courtroom defending some second-rate insurance company that took three months to pay his bills. He detested his job. He was having a sexual relationship with a married judge of Industrial Claims before whom he was trying cases. Of course he was winning those cases for the insurance companies and she could claim that she was a "conservative judge." It was a source of growing tension. She wasn't letting go so fast and he was sorry that he had gotten involved. She called at all times of night, when her older husband was asleep, begging for him to be more loving and caring and to spend more time together. Also, she was nothing much in bed. It had grown boring for him. It was almost an annoying routine. No excitement any more. He was thinking, "How do I get out of this?"

Mathews knew that I had seen them together having cocktails and dining in some small unusual places in North Miami Beach, far removed from where either of them lived or had offices. One didn't have to be a Sherlock Holmes to figure out what was going on. I tried to avoid both of them. Ultimately their affair went on its way out of my thinking. When it occasionally came into my thoughts I started to feel sorry for Mathews.

Who would think that an attorney would have to be a black-belt fighter in order to survive as a trial lawyer? Much to my surprise I learned from John Mathews that hand-to-hand combat often was part of being an attorney and trying a case. There seems to be no screening for mental stability at any stage, including admission to law school and the State and even Federal Bar Associations. If there were, Mathews could never have passed it. His psychiatric condition would have been treated as a confidential illness. Mathews isn't alone by far. The practice is loaded with nuts. They are dangerous. These violent wackos are often successful by intimidating everyone, including the judge.

In the middle of a hotly contested workers' compensation hearing before Judge Henderson, my opposing counsel John Mathews cracked up and announced that he was going to go out in the hall with me to resolve our differences by "beating the hell" out of me.

"Ress, I'm going to teach you a lesson." (He was shaking all over, in an uncontrollable rage.) "I'm going to bash you. Let's go outside and settle this thing right now."

The judge didn't even blink. He just sat there as if it was the customary thing to do.

I wasn't going anywhere with Mathews who was six inches taller and one hundred pounds heavier and ten years younger than I and clearly out of control. "Just sit tight, Lewis, and this too shall hopefully pass." And it did. But there was a lesson to be learned. The next associate that I hired had been a lineman on the

University of South Florida football team. He was about six four and weighed in at two eighty. David accompanied me to the next hearing I had with Mathews. I had him sit quietly in the back of the room. Sure enough, Mathews was losing and went berserk. He started on me again.

"O.K. Ress, Get up and come outside and we'll finish this. I'll punch you out."

"David, please get up and go outside with Mr. Mathews and accommodate him for me."

The judge said nothing. They were appointed. On salary... no waves. No overhead. No need to bring in business...Think of retirement...

David stood up and came forward. He was massive. Mathews took a good look at David and suddenly sat down and shut up. We finished trying the case without any further disruption and David became my "trial assistant."

Sometime later I saw a big, loaded .45 caliber revolver in Mathew's briefcase. He was nuts enough to use it. At any rate the lady judge, who ultimately divorced her husband, went onward and upward to a seat on the Circuit Court and Mathews retired to a small town in central Florida.

David, my trial assistant and bodyguard, is a good lawyer and he was assigned his own cases and I was back alone trying a hotly contested claim in front of Judge Leonard Barone. This time it was another nutcake, Boyd Tabacca. I had objected to some evidence he was trying to introduce and the judge ruled in my favor. There were just three of us in the hearing room. Tabacca was frustrated. He was really upset and he blurted out:

"Ress you goddamn Jew!"

Judge Barone was pretty cool. He said:

"Mr. Tabacca there is no place in this courtroom for that type of outburst."

Trying to be "Mr. Nice Guy" I said: "Judge I'm sure Mr. Tabacca just got carried away and he really doesn't mean that."

Tabacca: "Ress, you goddamn Jew bastard, I meant every word of it."

Tabacca jumps up from his chair and runs behind the judge and rushes towards me. He has passed by the seated judge and is just about to pounce on me. He weighs over two hundred pounds and I weigh in at about one forty-three. Did you ever see an old-fashioned lion tamer? I grabbed my chair and lifted it up so that the legs faced Tabacca. The judge jumped up, threw his arms around Tabacca, grabbing him from behind and subdued him.

Judge Barone adjourned the hearing. Tabacca stormed out and shouted:

"I'll get you, Ress."

"Judge, I'm not about to let this go unreported. The Florida Bar should know about this. I'm going to press charges."

"Lewis, Please don't do this. I'll be called as a witness. I will be blamed for not controlling my courtroom and it will reflect poorly on me. I would appreciate your not making any formal complaints."

What do I do? I wasn't going to let Tabacca get away with it.

Tabacca practiced workers' compensation law and the issues always involved medical testimony. I knew all of the orthopedists and neurosurgeons in the area and many of them were Jewish. The others all had close dealings with the Jewish community. It wasn't long before just about every orthopedist and neurosurgeon in the county had heard the story. They were no longer willing to be helpful to his clients and not easily available to testify for Mr. Tabacca. They wouldn't meet with him to discuss any cases. One of the doctors confronted him at a deposition.

"Oh –You're Tabacca, the anti-Semite. Get out of here."

I didn't say anything other than to the doctors, but Tabacca stopped getting cases referred from Jewish attorneys.

The last I heard about Mr. Tabacca was that he was up on charges before the Florida Bar for disciplinary action for soliciting oral sex from a client.

*   *   *   *   *

And one more confrontation:

Now that I am old and gray one would expect kindness, compassion for my failing mental acuity and some kind of respect, but the last mediation I attended was another wild experience. The electric company's truck had plowed into our client's car and caused quite a bit of damage. Our young pregnant client, Myra, had been injured and the utility company wanted to settle the case. Because of my age, I had referred the case to a trial specialist, Mel Martin, and he had reasons to see the matter resolved. We agreed to mediate.

The mediator was an older man, with thinning hair, a typical middle-level partner of a small firm. The office was plain. The furniture was plain. The mediator was plain.

The mediator introduced himself, told us of his experience and little else. He seemed to know the electric company's attorney on a first-name basis as well as the lady adjuster representing the electric company. The three of them had been speaking as we entered the glassed in conference room and I noticed that the conversation suddenly stopped. I sat next to our client, Myra. The mediator briefly explained the process. He told everyone that mediation was an informal procedure and asked them to listen to one another and to compromise in an effort to settle the case. He invited the attorneys to make opening statements. Our attorney, Mel Martin, was brief. He was seated and faced and addressed the mediator. He outlined the history of the accident, the extent of the injuries and resulting disability and agreed that we were there to attempt to settle the damages in a fair and reasonable way.

The next one to talk after Mel was the electric company's attorney, Del Johnson. He was a big guy, about six feet three inches, about sixty years old. He stood up over our client, facing and glaring down at our client, this one hundred pound, twenty-one-year-old. Instead of talking to the mediator about the facts he turned on our young girl, who was literally shaking in her boots, and raised his voice.

"I like mediation because it gives me a chance to talk directly to the plaintiff. You can't stop me. Young lady. I am going to make your life very difficult. I am going to cross-examine you on the witness stand. You will not be happy when I'm done. Do you want to go through that type of experience? You had better settle this case here and now. You make the decisions. You don't need to follow your attorney's instructions."

Before he could say anything more, and seeing that my co-counsel hadn't opened his mouth, I interrupted.

"Enough! Mr. Johnson, you should be making your remarks to the mediator and to us as attorneys. This is not a free-for-all where you can intimidate our client. We won't permit it. You address the issues to the mediator and stop harassing this young lady."

"Ress, don't you tell me what I can do. You come outside and I'll take care of you."

The mediator didn't say a word. He sat there impassively. It occurred to me that his firm was probably mediating many cases for the same electric company and their representative was sitting there absorbing everything.

The mediator finally said that Mr. Johnson should proceed, and he was soon back at it and I was again objecting. My co-counsel pulled me aside.

"Lewis, it's clear that this guy wants to see this settlement destroyed. Their last offer is really acceptable, but I'm trying to get them to increase it a bit. Our client makes a lousy witness. Our own doctor is balking at giving a permanent disability rating. Let's not blow the settlement over a personal dispute."

I physically escorted Myra out of the room when she started to cry. Mr. Johnson asked that she be compelled to return. The mediator evidently felt that Johnson had accomplished his mission. We went back and forth over the settlement amount. When we rejected the electric company's "final" offer Mr. Johnson was called outside the conference room to speak to the company representative and the mediator.

Mr. Johnson stuck his head in the door and called out:

"Ress, come out here and I'll settle this with you right now!"

Bullies are very much the same. They never go after

someone if they might not have a big advantage. I'm eighty-seven years old and around five feet six inches. This guy was at least fifteen years younger, almost a foot taller and about a hundred pounds heavier. The facts were against him. The law was against him. He was a miserable person, bellicose, mumbling, nasty, just completely angry, and emotionally unfit to be an attorney, so the best he could do was fistfight.

There's usually a way of getting even. I very quietly told the electric company's representative that we couldn't negotiate with Mr. Johnson because he was so insulting and that if they wanted to settle the case she would have to deal with us directly, alone. No attorney. No mediator. We settled in a matter of minutes. She told us initially that she had "full authority" to settle for our demand. Now she had to call the home office for settlement authority. She got it. They lie.

After the case was resolved Mr. Johnson could be heard in the hallway calling out for a physical battle with me, calling out personal insults to me.

"Come out here and fight. I'll punch you out, you old man!"

I was afraid to go out. The guy was nuts. My co-counsel, Mel Martin, prevailed upon me not to file a Bar or ethics complaint against Johnson. Mel didn't want to be involved. Johnson is thinking of retiring. The sooner, the better.

Even worse was the corrupt mediator, who allowed Johnson to run wild and failed to control the mediation. Why? The supposedly independent mediator will, privately, but in front of your client, tell you all of the shortcomings of your case and then ask that you divulge, in confidence, the least amount your client would accept as a settlement. This mediator sought our confidential trust and yet he failed to reveal that he repeatedly mediates for the same defendant electric company, deals with the same company's professional negotiators and attorneys regularly, gets instructions from them as to the amount they would like to see the case resolved for, tries to "bring it in" for less and even gives them wholesale discounted mediation fees. That explains his behavior. Without disclosing it, he's working for the other side. So much for integrity!

Two weeks after the case was settled Myra called me asking if I could help her cut down Mel Martin's attorney fee.

8

You Can't Win 'em All

Dry cleaning

My wife decided to send two sport coats and a suit of mine to the dry cleaners. The dry cleaners picked them up and gave her a receipt. That was the last we ever heard of them. After two months getting nowhere with the dry cleaning company, my wife filed a claim with our homeowner's insurance company. They opened a file, but nothing more. They wanted the purchase bills for the clothing.

"If you won't sue them, then I'll sue them all in Small Claims Court."

And so she did.

"Darling you're on your own with your case. I would just forget about it because of the time, effort, stress and bother of a Small Claims Court trial. I doubt that you'll get the full, new re-placement value."

"Those jackets and suit were worth a significant amount and no one will even talk to me."

My wife filed a "do-it-yourself" lawsuit against the dry cleaner, "Artistic Cleaners," and the homeowner's insurance company, "Royal Oak." They each, through an employee, offered her a fifty-dollar settlement because the clothes were old and she couldn't produce a bill for their purchase. I kept my distance. This was her case. She claimed the fair replacement value was five hundred dollars.

She prepared for trial by getting ads and prices for similar clothing from the stores where the clothes had been purchased a number of years before. She went over her case in her mind. No offers other than a total of one hundred dollars were made. So she went to trial.

On the day of the trial at about eleven in the morning my secretary told me that the presiding senior judge of the Small Claims Court was on the phone.

"Lewis, you're really going to enjoy this. I'm sitting on a dry cleaning case involving your wife. She is suing "Artistic", the dry cleaner, who says that you are his attorney. She's also suing your homeowner's insurance company, "Royal Oak" and they are also telling me that you are their attorney. What do you want me to do?"

I was taken totally by surprise.

"Judge, I'll tell you what: rule in favor of my wife, but tell the dry cleaner and the insurance adjuster to call me right away."

It didn't take fifteen minutes and the dry cleaner was on the phone.

"What is it with your wife, Lewis?"

"Hold up Bernie, Take a deep breath. Pay Esta the $250.00 and take $500.00 off my outstanding bill and don't say anything to her."

"Lewis, you are a mensch."

Another five minutes goes by and the Royal Oak adjuster is on the phone.

"I know. I know... Pay my wife $250.00 and take $500.00 off any one of my outstanding bills. No... Really... It's my pleasure."

That night my wife greeted me:

"So you think you're the only lawyer in the family. I won! I'm getting two hundred and fifty dollars from each of them and they even shook my hand when we left the courthouse."

"Keep the money, darling, you earned it."

I did finally tell her the whole story. It's better that way than to risk a happy marriage.

9

The Tale of the Frozen Pussy

"Mr. Ress, it's Mrs. Burnside on the phone."

"Darling, I have to see you right away."

She was an attractive dental wife, blue eyes, blond hair, designer dresses and her husband was an outstanding member of the dental society. She sat down across from my desk and was in obvious distress. A lace handkerchief was at her eyes.

She gave me a man's name.

"Dr. Wasserman…" and then said:

"He froze my Pussy without my permission."

What a case! Her Persian cat, "Pussy" had a history of heart problems. She had taken it to the vet for a clipping and bath. Evidently while the cat was being bathed it suffered a heart attack and died. Ellie learned of the cat's fate through a very short, clipped phone call from the doctor's office.

"Your cat died while getting a bath. Do you want us to dispose of the remains or you may pick them up."

The doctor refused to take her phone calls. No doctor, no office manager, no explanation.

"The doctor treated me like dirt. No phone call. No offer to have an office meeting, nor any real explanation. No sympathy!

At least I want an apology."

The story was even more heartrending. When Ellie went to the vet's office to pick up the remains, the secretary brought out a cold, hard object in a plain dark plastic bag.

"My Pussy was hard as a rock."

He had frozen her Pussy without her permission! No doctor came out to talk to her. No office manager. No explanation and no apology.

"What if they sedated my cat, without remembering that it had a heart condition?"

The next thing Ellie learned was that an autopsy could not be performed on a frozen cat.

What can the family lawyer do? I tried calling the doctor. He wouldn't talk to me. I wrote to the doctor. No reply.

The last resort was a lawsuit, which I filed in the Dade County Circuit Court, with unlimited jurisdiction. An insurance defense firm filed an appearance and the standard Motion to Dismiss. The Judge's administrative assistant issued an Order under the Judge's name for a suit conference at the Judge's Chambers with all parties to be present.

The day and time arrived and Ellie and I climbed the marble steps to the Courthouse. I remember her heels clicking on the marble floor. Up the bronze-doored elevator we went to the eleventh floor. Dr. Wasserman was there with his attorney. They did not even say "hello."

The judge's chambers were in a large office with a long table and a cross-table at the end. After a short wait the secretary ushered us in and we sat on one side of the long table with the doctor and his attorney glaring at us from the other side. The Judge's high back-chair was on a raised platform. He entered, fully robed, from a side door and walked rapidly to his chair.

"Now what is this all about, Mr. Ress"

"Your Honor, this man froze my client's Pussy without her permission!"

I swear to God – I really said it.

The judge grabbed quickly for his face. His hands covered his mouth. His eyes rolled into his head. His face reddened and he slid under the table, right down from his high-backed chair. He coughed, sputtered, recovered himself, sat up and leaned over.

"Mr. Ress, What do you want?"

"An apology your Honor."

The doctor stood up at the table and said: "Never."

The Judge struck the table with his gavel. The noise sounded like a clap of thunder. The judge stared at the doctor.

"Apologize NOW!"

The doctor says:

"I'm sorry."

"That's not enough your Honor. It has to be meaningful. He has to say he's sorry for the way he treated my client."

"I'm sorry. I didn't mean to offend you. I apologize for the way you were treated."

"Ellie, is that acceptable to you?

"Yes."

Case dismissed!

What's left? A moral: "Never freeze a lady's pussy without her permission."

* * * * *

What else is left? My fee.
How do you set a fee?

My fee was the exclusive rights to this story.

10

Position of the Lion

Mrs. Ann D'Angelo was just like a nun. I knew this because I had been representing the diocese of Miami for about five years at this time. Anyhow, this mild, quiet, thin, fifty-five-year-old single, graying lady, who wore black dresses, long black stockings, black shoes with low heels, tied her hair back with a black ribbon, and wore black-rimmed glasses, had been in an automobile accident and had been recommended to me by her local priest. It was hard to get any information out of her. She spoke softly and hesitatingly.

"I am in some pain in my low back, but I am doing well and I am back to work. Please see if you can settle my case."

I tried, but the insurance company's attorney was not going to recommend one penny to settle. He was Joe Stanton, a partner in the "Sams" law firm, the most competent, aggressive plaintiff's lawyers in town. When a plaintiff's lawyer gets a defense case—watch out. They go wild. They are tougher, harder and meaner by far than the regular defense boys. They give nothing. They love the idea of appearing in court for the "other side."

The case had been around for a while and was coming up for trial. The defendant, Fred Wilson, was an older man who was on his way home from the gas station when he entered the intersection. He said that he stopped at the stop sign and started across the street when my client, driving an old Ford, struck his car. He had looked to the right, up the entire street, before entering the intersection. He saw her coming, but had more than enough time to cross the road. She actually put on speed and crashed into him. It was "all her fault."

Mr. Wilson said that although he did not get out of his car, he saw Mrs. D'Angelo at the scene and that she was not injured.

"I was the one who was hurt. My arthritis kicked up terribly and I was treated for my neck and back for over a month."

Of course, Mrs. D'Angelo had quite a different story. She said that she was driving home from church and Mr. Wilson's brown Pontiac pulled out right in front of her. "He never stopped or even slowed down at the stop sign." She had back pain right then and there and complained to the police about it, but never went to the hospital. Three days later, the same priest who had recommended me sent her to Dr. Ortiz.

Dr. Arturo Ortiz was a mostly defense-oriented orthopedic surgeon. He was short, partially bald, with eyeglasses, pleasant, refined, fairly low keyed and well respected. He had treated her for over six months with physical therapy, for a low-back sprain with pain going down her right leg. The medical bill was over two thousand dollars with x-rays, injections to the low back, heat therapy and massage. He hadn't prepared a final report.

When I spoke to Dr. Ortiz, he said:

"Lewis, I would like to help you out, but there is little or nothing here. I will hold up on the final report, but other than some mild muscle spasm there is nothing of a permanent nature to Mrs. D'Angelo'.'"

The defense doctor said that although Ann had some limitation of motion and consistent subjective complaints, she was exaggerating and he found no objective basis to assess any permanent disability.

There were absolutely no offers of settlement. In order to be entitled to a recovery we had to prove a permanent injury. The judge's clerk called.

"You are number one for Monday."

We had no choice. We met on Sunday afternoon at my office. We went over her testimony and I prepared her for cross-examination. I explained to her that all she had to do was tell the truth and that we had little or nothing to lose since the offer to settle was "zero." I didn't tell her that I was shaking in my pants because I couldn't prove any "permanency." So on Monday morning down to the courthouse Ann and I went. I was up against the wall. She was not happy, but we had no choice.

The courthouse was the tallest building in town at the time. It was built of white granite in the 1920s in anticipation of the growth of Miami. It had the large, wide-set of steps in the front, with the Greek columns and marble floors. I always think of the floors because they caused all kinds of clicking and clacking when women walked there. The elevators had engraved bronze doors. On the top floor there was a jail and the Sheriff's office. The floors below held the courtrooms and below those were the clerks' and the property tax offices. Our trial was to be heard in the main courtroom, which was two stories high, paneled in dark wood, with elevated platforms for the judge, jury and witness stand. There were about twenty rows of seats for the audience and the tall windows were draped in heavy fabric. It was an intimidating place. Mrs. D'Angelo was frightened.

"Mr. Ress, can't we settle? I don't want to testify."

There was Joe Stanton standing next to his client, Mr. Wilson

"Joe, can I speak to you for a minute?"

"If you are talking about settlement, the answer is—not a penny. I'm going to whip you in this case!"

Mr. Wilson was smirking. I was left with no alternative. I had no choice.

We interviewed the jury and exercised our challenges. We made opening statements. I was intentionally vague because I didn't know what was going to come from the witness stand. We might only have Mrs. D'Angelo's unsubstantiated, subjective complaints to establish the required permanent disability.

Mrs. D'Angelo testified about the accident and her injuries and limitations. Joe Stanton realized that a tough cross-examination could backfire, so he was pretty gentle with her. He did bring out that a person driving Mr. Wilson's car could, by just turning his head all the way to the right, see all the way up the road to where she was driving. She admitted that the view was unobstructed.

Dr. Ortiz had not shown up at the time he was due. I asked for a brief recess and called his office.

"Mr. Ress, Dr. Ortiz has been held up in emergency surgery, but he'll be there, although he mentioned to me that he didn't think you would really want him to testify."

"If you contact him please tell him that I need him at the courtroom right away."

I was shaking inside. What could I do? What was going to happen? How do I handle this? What could I say to Dr. Ortiz to change his mind? Over Stanton's objection, the Judge granted me leave to produce the doctor out of turn since he had been in emergency surgery.

Mr. Wilson took the stand for the defense. He gave the same story as before almost as though it was rehearsed. My turn to cross-examine. I asked him simple questions to get him talking and then I got into his story about how the accident happened. I gradually positioned myself to his right and slightly behind where he was sitting in the witness chair. I don't know what made me do this, but I don't like to stand still when I am speaking in the courtroom. Mr. Wilson now had questions coming from his right side, a little behind him.

"Mr. Wilson, why don't you face me when I ask you my questions?

"Mr. Ress, you know that I have arthritis and cannot turn my head to the right at all. I have to turn my entire body."

"Then you cannot turn your head to the right?"

"No."

I thought to myself: Stop there! Don't belabor it. You got what you want. Don't give him the opportunity to explain it away.

"No further questions, your Honor."

Dr. Ortiz had entered the rear door of the courtroom. He gave me a sheepish look and then looked down. He held a small office file in his hand.

"Your Honor, may I have three minutes to talk to Dr. Ortiz before I put him on?"

"Granted."

"Art, I am desperate. Can't you help me even a little? Isn't there something my client cannot do."

"She can't have sex in the position of the lion."

"Take the stand."

I qualified the doctor, who had testified for Joe Stanton in the past, and he described the history and treatment. Then came the key question:

"As a result of the injuries sustained in this accident is there any activity in which Mrs. D'Angelo is unable to engage?"

Well, neither I nor the jury had any idea of what having sex in the position of the lion was, but for thirty minutes the conservative orthopedist clearly and methodically described it in detail. The jury was leaning out over their seats in rapt attention. Mrs. D'Angelo was blushing. Joe Stanton was in a state of shock. Dr. Ortiz made eye contact with the jurors. He spoke distinctly and without any accent.

"The woman gets on all fours—that is, on her hands and knees. The man mounts her from behind, that is, from the rear. There are certain nerves involved that enhance the pleasure of penetration from this position, but in Mrs. D'Angelo's case would cause her exquisite pain. Yes Mr. Ress, the pain to Mrs. D'Angelo would be exquisite…. (etc., etc.)."

Joe Stanton couldn't think of any questions to ask Dr. Ortiz without making the situation worse.

We had closing argument and I went to town. I jumped on Mr. Wilson's inconsistent sworn testimony.

"How could he have looked up and down that street, when he can't turn his head to the right? He tried to mislead us. He lied to us! He lied under oath!"

Then I stressed Mrs. D'Angelo's future pain.

"We all heard Dr. Ortiz, a respected orthopedic specialist, describe the lengthy treatment and painful experience suffered by Mrs. D'Angelo and her future of exquisite pain caused by this injury…"

The case was over and we waited for the verdict. No matter how experienced you are, it is a crazy, stressful time with no one knowing what the outcome will be. I couldn't believe that Dr. Ortiz came up with that testimony. My client had blushed and had been clearly embarrassed by it, but the jury had paid rapt attention. They were envisioning the "position of the lion" and my meek client being the sex object.

After three hours the judge's clerk called out: "Mr. Ress, please come into the courtroom, the jury has reached a verdict."

"We the jury find for the plaintiff and award damages in the amount of fifty thousand dollars. So say we all."

11

Change of Venue

The teenage high school football star was killed in the crash. His girlfriend was severely injured. The red Porsche sports car that struck their Chevrolet Bel Air was going about eighty-five miles an hour in a thirty-five mile an hour speed zone. It was being driven by the GEICO heir, Leo Goodwin III, who, now in his early twenties, was known to be a heavy drug user and had caused at least two other accidents as a result of his irresponsible driving. One of them involved his Ferrari 308 GTB V-8, which he'd crashed into a parked camper. In fact, Judge Fischer was considering him to be a public nuisance and as such would prohibit him from driving in Broward County. Over one thousand citizens had signed a petition to stop Leo from driving, but the kid continued to drive, do drugs, chase women and hang around in bars, one of which was in a yacht club just on the other side of the Seventeenth Street causeway, opposite the Pier 66 hotel. When he was on probation he left the country and toured Europe.

The insurance company wouldn't tender the basic policy limits and the excess or umbrella carrier wasn't tendering their million in additional insurance coverage. They were denying liability, claiming that Leo's foot slid off a poorly designed clutch pedal. When we filed suit they moved to have the case tried in Naples, over in Collier County where jury verdicts were the lowest in Florida. Thus the trial within a trial, like a play within a play, occurred. The courtroom was packed.

"Your Honor, we respectfully move the Court to change the venue of this case to Naples, Florida, and in partial support would show the Court that Leo Goodwin III is not able to have a fair trial in Broward County, due to the enormous publicity of a disparaging nature which had permeated this community. Why, every day and night the newspapers, particularly the *Sun Sentinel*, and the television channels, particularly CBS and NBC, have filled the community with a hatred for our client so severe that a fair and impartial trial is out of the question...."

"Your Honor, I represent the plaintiffs in this matter and it is our position that there should be no problem in seating a fair and independently minded jury. Unless we seat jurors and voire dire (question) them we don't know that a proper jury cannot be found. The plaintiffs are entitled to have their case heard where the present jurisdiction lies and the defense must prove by a preponderance of evidence that an objective jury cannot be found. Unless and until we actually place jurors in the box we'll never be able to say that a fair jury could not be found."

As we left the courthouse, at least five reporters, two television camera teams and a group of Goodwin haters, who I believed were created and encouraged by the defense, surrounded me. Flashbulbs were going off. Bright TV lights were on and I was gently saying that we had "No comment."

The next day a new amendment to the Motion to Change Venue was filed, and the headlines and articles from the *Sun*

Sentinel and the TV Nightly News reports were transcribed and attached as further evidence that a fair trial in Fort Lauderdale was impossible.

Back to court for another hearing. It was hearing number three and this was just relating to the adverse publicity. This time I asked permission to address the Court and turned toward the crowded spectators.

"All of you who are from the media, the newspapers and television stations raise your hands."

Almost every hand went up.

"Counsel, what are you doing? You can't take over my courtroom."

"Judge, I just want you to see that this has become a media event in and of itself. Tomorrow you will read about this hearing in the newspapers and it will be on TV and on the radio and a new amended motion will be filed. It will continue until you rule."

"Get on with it, gentlemen. Let's consider the polls you wish to present."

The GEICO attorneys put two experts on the stand. Each was from a well-known professional polling company. They had employees take a telephone poll of fifty persons during the six o'clock mealtime and eighty percent stated that they would like to see Leo Goodwin III hanging by his neck from the nearest large tree or words to that effect. My experience was that in situations like this they took many polls using different employees until they got the results they wanted, then the unfavorable polls and the people that took them sort of disappeared.

We were allowed to respond. I called my cute, petite receptionist to the stand. Little Doris had taken a poll at my request calling fifty people at random from the telephone book all of who lived in different parts of Fort Lauderdale. She brought her records and notes with her and testified that hardly any of the persons she polled even knew of Leo Goodwin III and not one of them knew of the pending trial. All of them said that they had no opinion as to this case. They didn't know that it was going on. She was so pretty and spoke in such a sweet and naïve voice that the defense didn't try to cross-examine her. Actually we had discarded five prior polls taken by other secretaries that expressed the general hatred of Leo Goodwin III.

The next day the headlines, TV and radio screamed: "Goodwin defense polls show fair trial impossible."

Hearing number four covered their psychiatrist who was an assistant professor. His name had been listed as an expert and I had plenty of time to check him out and get my own psychiatrist. Their witness, Professor Black, was a Board-Certified, Florida State University, medically trained specialist. He was a professional witness who made the better part of his living as a trial expert. He advertised his availability. I checked his research background and looked for any articles he may have written on the venue-change subject. Nothing. Then I went at it the back way by looking for change of venue cases to see if he had ever testified in them. Sure enough, he had testified for the famous plaintiffs' attorney Murray Sams in a Miami change of venue case. The testimony had never been transcribed.

What would he be doing testifying for Murray who was also trying to stop being transferred to Naples? He was testifying for the exact opposite side he was now helping! I found the court reporter, Jerry Schwartz, and he was able to find the transcript.

Now I was listening to this whore swear that Goodwin could never get a fair trial and quoting all of the phony statistics to support this conclusion. His testimony followed his report almost word for word and concluded:

"It is my considered opinion, within the realm of medical and psychiatric probability, based on the huge amount of adverse publicity and the polls and the lynch atmosphere in this community directed against him, that Mr. Goodwin can never get a fair or objective trial in this venue of Broward County, Florida."

The Goodwin attorneys turned to me and said:

"Your witness."

Boy, was he going to be my witness. I started off gently, going over the number of times he had testified as an expert, his fees, his advertising. Just enough to get him irritated to where he was looking to get me. Then I said:

"Dr. Black, allow to me ask your opinion of the following." And I recited…

"All the polls claiming prejudice in a Change of Venue case are meaningless. All the testimony of experts talking about publicity requiring a Change of Venue is a sham. Scientifically there is no way to say that a community is so tilted that a fair trial cannot be had. Unless and until a jury is impaneled no one who is responsible can say that a case should be removed to another jurisdiction. I stake my professional reputation on this."

"Do you agree with that? What are your comments?"

Dr. Black took the bait and swallowed the hook.

"Mr. Ress, that is the biggest liar in the world saying that. That statement is just untrue. It is inaccurate, totally incorrect, misleading, unscientific and had to come from a total imbecile. No I certainly do not agree with it."

"Dr. Black, do you remember testifying in the 'Arbiter' case for Murray Sams in Miami? You did testify in that case didn't you? (*silence*) I have the official court reporter standing outside this courtroom. That was your expert testimony that I quoted. YOU said those things after being sworn and under oath!"

There was dead silence. Black couldn't get out of it.

"How did you find that?"

Then he was gone.

The Judge said: "I've heard enough. Motion to Change Venue is denied."

There was a rush to the door and the flashbulbs started going off. The reporters pressed and I finally said:

"I think we'll get a fair trial here in Fort Lauderdale."

Tom Randall, Goodwin's lead attorney came up to me.

"Lewis, we're tendering the first million dollars. That's our policy limit. Bill Harris is in his office and is expecting you. They have more."

Harris tendered the balance.

Believe it or not GEICO stock wasn't worth very much at the time and Leo was only standing in line to inherit. He had nothing in his own name. His father the sixty million dollar tycoon was facing bankruptcy.

Leo Goodwin III didn't learn much. He never apologized or repented. He was twenty-five years old when he died of a drug overdose.

12

L-1011

I. The Crash

The sky was black. The ground was black. No lights. No beacons. No way to tell up from down. Eastern Airlines Lockheed-1011, the newest, most sophisticated, most advanced airliner of the time, was over the Everglades, the black swamps, heading for the Miami International Airport. Everything was dark, black, dead, lifeless. There was no horizon. The crew was preparing for landing about seventy miles to the west of Miami. They were protected by radar, electronic sensors, altimeters, every conceivable scientific device to assure the safety of the plane. The front lock wheel light didn't go on. The wheels were supposed to be down, or were they? The pilot, Bob Loft, put the plane on "autopilot." They would check to see if the wheels were down. Maybe the bulb was out. Evidently one of the crew accidentally turned off the autopilot, possibly brushing against it, and the L-1011 descended. There was no "up" or "down". There was just black and death. They slammed into the swamp at midnight, about twenty miles out. The plane broke apart. About one hundred and seventy five people were on the L-1011. There were families on vacation, little children. Seventy-four lived.

Tom McDermott survived the explosion and the black cold waters. It was late December, 1972. He was strapped in and found himself sinking, dazed, bloody. He was bleeding from his skull. He was bleeding from a slice on this right leg. Half his clothes were torn off. With extreme effort he fought to stay conscious, released his seatbelt and started to swim away from the wreckage. The helicopters came in after what seemed to be a long, long time of fighting to stay awake. The blood was in his eyes. The water was black and cold. His legs were numb. The screaming and shouting were eerie. It was dark. No lights. No flashlights. It was living hell. Was someone singing Christmas carols?

They finally found him, dazed, shaking and mumbling incoherently. They picked him up in an airboat and he was helicoptered to Jackson Memorial Hospital. The airboat guys had been out gigging frogs and kept bringing the survivors to the helicopters despite their own injuries. The doctors never told Tom how many stitches they put into his scalp and his leg. Try over fifty in the skull and a hundred in the leg.

The recovery was slow and during this time Tom contacted me about representing him. The first problem was that he was an employee of Eastern Airlines, flying on a pass. He might be limited to workers' compensation, since Eastern claimed that he was in the course of his employment.

In the meantime his wounds became infected from the exposure to swamp water and the infections became worse and worse. It was gas gangrene from that swamp water. Tom wound up in the hyperbaric chamber, being treated with pure oxygen. He could only say that it was like being trapped in a coffin. There was a feeling of suffocation. The sides of the chamber kept crushing in and one couldn't get out. The scars would be forever, both inside and out.

It took a Motion to Dismiss the workers' compensation claim file and a convincing argument to allow Tom to keep his liability claim against Eastern. But I decided not to file a lawsuit and to await the National Transportation Safety Board (NTSB) investigation report. Others had filed in Federal Court, and the Judge had determined that those who filed were in a "class action." He appointed a committee of attorneys to investigate the cause of the crash, including John Appleton from New York City and Irwin Polite from Miami. Irwin was a well-known air-crash specialist and a perfect gentleman. We didn't join the McDermott claim with them. We never filed a lawsuit and never used their investigation for advancing our claim. My contingent attorneys' fee would be substantially less if our case was settled without having filed a lawsuit, which was fine with me.

The NTSB issued its report. Pilot error! The Captain, Bob Loft, with thirty-two years of experience and almost thirty thousand air hours, had, after placing the L-1011 on automatic pilot, accidentally leaned on the yoke, which then automatically released the automatic pilot. What happens is that when the pilot lets go of the yoke the automatic pilot immediately takes over and maintains the same course as when the pilot released it. If the yoke is then touched again it goes back on manual, turning off the automatic pilot. Then the plane had no control and started down. In addition there was the failure of the crew to notice the instruments including a speaker altitude alert. The TriStar

Whisperliner, almost brand new, started its descent unnoticed by the crew.

One day the phone rang. I had filed a claim with Eastern's attorneys and it was Dick Thurman, the senior partner of a large downtown defense firm. I guess in those days we attorneys were kinder and trusted one another. It was another example of the "high road."

"Lewis, this is Dick Thurman. I am instructed to settle the McDermott case. Just tell me what you want and I'll try to get it. We've accepted liability."

They accepted our offer and McDermott was "in the chips." What he did with his money is surprising. I was glad to get a rather significant fee, two hundred and fifty thousand dollars, since it was thirty-three percent of the total recovery. However, the next thing I knew the Federal Court served me with a Court Order, determining, without a hearing, that my fee was subject to the Court taking a significant portion of it and awarding it to the judge's committee, namely twenty-five percent, which came to about sixty-two thousand dollars.

I filed a Motion for Relief and appeared "specially" stating that I was not subject to the Court's jurisdiction and was not subjecting myself to it now. We had never filed a lawsuit and certainly weren't a part of the "class" that was suing and before the court. We were not in this court and had no duty or obligation to anyone to share our fees for our independent settlement of this case. We were being deprived of our rights to our property unconstitutionally and without "due process." The judge leaned over said:

"You received the benefit of the committee's work."

"Judge, Your Honor, I respectfully don't think so. I relied on the NTSB investigation and it wasn't until after Eastern received its report that they settled with us, out of Court."

"Pay the committee twenty-five percent of your fee. It is so ordered."

We appealed.

The appeal went to the Fifth District Federal Court of Appeals in New Orleans. In the meantime I placed my entire fee in a special trust account since the Appellate Court might even award more than the Federal District Judge. My brief was fairly emotional. The United States Constitution prohibits taking of property without "due process." The Court had no jurisdiction over me. The committee's work was unknown to me and never used by me. Eastern settled based on the government investigation, which found Eastern responsible.

I found out that I wasn't the only one in this appeal. Mine was joined by about six other attorneys who were similarly having portions of their fee awarded to the committee attorneys. I was sorry I wasn't on the committee. They were in line to collect a bundle.

It was a cold, dreary day in New Orleans. It was teeming. Umbrellas were inadequate. There I was in this huge marble federal appeals courthouse. It was like a Greek temple. I felt very small. I was walking down the wide hallway, dripping from the rain, shaking my umbrella and looking for the courtroom when a gentleman approached me.

"Are you Lewis Ress? I'm John Appleton. Do you want to settle this case?"

"Mr. Appleton, I'm honored to meet you and I know

whatever my claims of injustice, they weren't instigated by you. You enjoy a fine reputation."

I had deposited my entire fee in a bank trust account. It had been earning high interest for almost two years. The interest alone was over fifteen thousand dollars.

"Lewis, you have the strongest case of the group and I would be glad to let you go home. How about twelve thousand dollars?"

"Done."

The Appellate Court ruled. They found that it was quite all right for the District Judge to appoint a committee and award whatever fees he deemed appropriate and to take a portion of these fees from attorneys who were not before the court since they benefited from the committee's efforts. If I had not settled I would have tried to get the attention of the U.S. Supreme Court, but I don't think they are thrilled with the thought of protecting attorneys' fees.

II. The Aftermath

McDermott was a six-foot four-inch Irish-American with a great sense of humor and a kind and pleasant attitude, about fifteen years younger than I. He was really a "good guy." When he first retained me he said:

"OK, Ress, you'll represent me, get your fee and you'll be gone. You'll never bother with me again."

I don't know what came over me, but I answered:

"That won't be so. Tom, we'll become friends and I will be your friend for life."

It was a foolish thing to say. One of those statements that seemed hollow and meaningless. A promise to someone I hardly knew. We had little in common, but there was something genuine about Tom and it came through and could be sensed just by being around him, watching him, listening to him. He was a straight talker. I enjoyed him. He was truly celebrating his life.

Tom loved to fish and he took his money and bought three fishing boats, one of them, a party fishing boat over sixty feet long. It was called the "Royal Fleet." They were docked at the Howard Johnson's Motel down in Key Largo. For a while Tom did quite well. He kept his job at Eastern Airlines and became a weight balancer, checking the freight and its distribution in the cargo hold. He kept sending me injured Eastern Airlines employees and I did quite well for them and for myself.

* * * * *

Colonel Frank Borman became the CEO of Eastern. He was a "no nonsense" military type. He was a test pilot, aeronautical engineer, and famous astronaut. He had been the commander of Gemini 7 and of course Apollo 8, which rode to the dark side of the moon. He also, unknown to many, had a Harvard Business School degree. He had raced from his home to the scene of the crash and helped rescue the injured. He ran a tight ship at Eastern and worked with the new CEO Frank Lorenzo to keep the company profitable and to control the unions. Frank Lorenzo was clearly anti-union and fired a number of mechanics, possibly with the idea of ultimately having a non-union company. Finally the head of the mechanics' union, who also had a power complex, instigated a strike against Eastern. Mr. Lorenzo, the CEO, would suffer no insurrection. They went head to head, these strong-willed men, and both lost. Eastern Airlines went bankrupt and never came out of it. No mergers. No compromises. No reorganization. All the Eastern employees lost their jobs. The mechanics would probably get other employment, but everyone lost retirement and seniority. It is said that Mr. Lorenzo walked away with seven hundred and fifty million dollars. The end result was that a major airline based in Miami was lost in great part due to conflicting egos.

* * * * *

Fortunately, Tom retired at the right time. As part of his retirement Tom would take one of his boats to the Bahamas and once I met him in Bimini and brought my younger son, Brad, who was sixteen. They hit it off and fished and did some serious beer drinking together. My wife liked Tom and when he remarried she took a liking to his new wife, so we saw them fairly regularly. As part of his dream retirement Tom moved to Key Largo and we used to go down to visit and to fish with him. His fishing rod was called "the Irish stick."

You know as well as I that economics isn't a science and the money road is bumpy. The economy drops and people stop paying to fish. It happened sort of gradually. I'm not sure how long it took, but things went downhill in the sport fishing industry and Tom lost his boats, even his own personal thirty-five footer on which he and his recent wife were living. The next thing I learned was that Tom wasn't doing so well. He was working as a bartender at Howard Johnson's.

* * * * *

Colonel Frank Borman retired and moved back to Arizona and then to New Mexico. I think he suffers from a sinus problem. He was born in 1928 and is still active. Captain Bob Loft was found to have a brain tumor at the time of the crash, but it was never determined that it contributed to the accident. He and flight engineer Don Ripo, who also died in the crash, have been sighted after the crash a number of times by a number of different former Eastern employees on other L-1011's. Their ghosts were thought to haunt that series of aircraft. There have been no reported sightings since the L-1011's went out of service and disappeared. Colonel Borman says "it's nonsense."

* * * * *

Tom was having his own ghost problems. He was seeing "little men." They were coming into his bedroom at night to visit him. Maybe they come from the swamps. His legs gradually stopped working, possibly from the damage caused by the crash. He was placed in a "rest home" in Naples, then finally was able to get into a nicer rehabilitation facility in Islamorada. He is back in the Keys. He's run out of money. He's still cheery and full of life. My wife and I keep my promise. We visit, make sure that he has money in his account and plenty of beer in his cooler.

Well, it's over now. Tom died just a few months ago. His heart must have given out. The funeral party took two boats out into the Atlantic. Tom's ashes were put inside a light brown biodegradable fiber container in the shape of a turtle. He was lowered onto the reef off of Key Largo. There was a lot of drinking.

13

"All Rise!"

Judge Samuel Halpert was the senior workers' compensation judge, about sixty years old, short, balding and well dressed. His office in the State Office Building on northwest Twelfth Avenue was elaborate; a big desk in the middle of a big carpeted sunlit room with three interview chairs, a sofa and lots of plants. It was connected to his spacious courtroom, which was about double the size of the other judges' who reported to him. There were seats for over fifty lawyers. Of course he sat on a raised platform presiding over everything that happened there. There was little doubt that he was a powerful man not to be trifled with.

I was about the last person to tangle with Judge Halpert. The Aetna Casualty had just referred a case to me involving widow's benefits being claimed by the surviving wife of a metalworker. She was representing herself, which we call "pro se." The claims adjuster was certain that she had not filed her claim on time and that it was barred by the Statute of Limitations, which required filing within two years of the accident. The claim had been properly contested by the insurance company.

After looking at the file and reading all of the supporting documents and considering all of the possible exceptions and extensions of the Statute of Limitations, the claim seemed to be clearly barred for failing to file on time. Maybe that's why she wasn't represented, since no lawyer would undertake the case. I spoke to the adjuster and suggested that since this was a widow I would waive my legal fee for filing the Motion to Dismiss, taking the widow's deposition, attending the hearing and drawing the Order of Dismissal, which would come to about two thousand dollars, and that we should give the money to the widow. I would draw the settlement papers without charge. It was difficult to convince the supervisor, but the Aetna finally agreed. After speaking to the widow and asking her as many questions relating to the possible delay in filing the claim that could create an excuse for late filing, it appeared to me that the claim was clearly barred. So I prepared the Petition for Lump Sum Washout Settlement and she signed it and was happy to be receiving two thousand dollars. It was submitted. All we needed was the written approval from Judge Halpert. That was two weeks ago and nothing was heard from the Judge, … until now

It was the Judge's secretary.

"Mr. Ress, Judge Halpert wants to see you now. Immediately! In his office. He means right now."

"Ress, you can remain standing." I was in front of the Judge in his Chambers. He was glowering at me. He was gruff as hell.

"What do you think you are trying to get away with? Two thousand dollars to settle a death case?"

"Judge, the Statute of Limitations has run and sir, the case has no value."

"Don't tell me about the Statute of Limitations. I've looked at this carefully and asked some of the other attorneys to do the same. We all believe that there are so many exceptions to the Statute of Limitations that you are abusing this widow. I'm going to have you disbarred for attempting to defraud this lady and this Court.

Now get out of here."

I was shaking. My vision was blurred. My mouth was dry and my voice was hoarse. What had I gotten into? Maybe he was right and I had not gone far enough in investigating the possible exceptions to the statute. There were many. It was impossible to work any more that day. The next day was as bad. I continued to be unable to work. Three sleepless nights and three miserable days followed. At night I tossed and turned, got out of bed and paced back and forth. What could it be? What did I miss? What would happen to me? I'd be disgraced. Everything I worked for would be lost. My clients, my practice, my reputation all ruined. What could I do? Go back over everything. Read all the cases describing exceptions to the time for filing. Read and reread the Aetna's file. Think. What could his group of attorneys have come up with? Was there anything that would extend the time for filing or excuse the late filing? I checked the date the claim was recorded at the Workers' Compensation Commission. Nothing…

"Mr. Ress, it's Judge Halpert's secretary on line two."

"Mr. Ress, Judge Halpert would like you to come down to his office as soon as possible."

"Lewis, Sit down. I owe you an apology. I checked the Statute of Limitations out personally, backwards and forwards, and you were right. I couldn't figure out why the insurance company was paying this lady two thousand dollars when all they had to do was file to dismiss. So I called the Aetna and learned that you had campaigned to give this widow the money and that it was coming from your attorney's fee, which you had waived. You are a gentleman and I am so sorry to have doubted you."

The next time I appeared in Judge Halpert's courtroom was on a different case. There were over thirty lawyers seated waiting for him.

"All rise…"

The Honorable Samuel Halpert, Senior Workers' Compensation Judge strode to his raised platform. He sat down and leaned forward addressing the attorneys.

"Gentlemen, I am making this statement in open court. I apologize to Mr. Ress. Anything Mr. Ress tells me in this courtroom hereafter will be accepted by me as 'fact.'"

What a relief. I thought that would be the end of it. Not so fast.

It wasn't over a week later that I was walking in the street at the corner nearest the State Office Building when Arnold Zalper, an older man, who had authored the latest textbook on workers' compensation, came up to me. He looked me straight in the eyes and said:

"You are a liar."

I was stunned. I barely knew Mr. Zalper. He usually was a quiet guy. I just didn't say anything. I didn't know what he was talking about. Maybe he was nuts and would become violent if I argued with him. I just stared back at him. He didn't say anything else. He just walked away.

Why would someone like Mr. Zalper turn on me? Why? What did I ever do to him? I never even had a case with him. I had no social contact with him. It finally dawned on me. Zalper wrote the book. Who would Judge Halpert go to for an opinion on the Statute of Limitations? And I knew that they were close friends. He must have been terribly embarrassed to learn that I was truthful and that he was wrong.

14

Superlawyers

"If you have to be a mediocrity, be the best one."
Kal Ress (my father)

What makes a "Superstar Lawyer?" Marketing is the answer, not great talent or meticulous work product. Superlawyers write books—which are usually ghostwritten. They lecture at educational seminars. The material is generally researched and prepared for them. They send out newsletters—which are written for them. They advertise in Bar journals, on billboards and especially on T.V., done through an advertising agency and boast about their successes. They promote themselves to become consultants for television stations. They use the internet and offer fact kits and materials to attorneys in order to seek referrals. Much of their solicitation is subcontracted to publicity consultants. Clerks cull out the financially rewarding cases and associates sign up the clients. They use dummy law firms and non-lawyers to solicit cases through television ads in phone-in phone numbers:

"If you have had complications from mesh surgery call us. You may have a claim for a large sum of money...

Operators are standing by...."
"To all former NFL football players. You may have a brain-dam-
age claim. Call us at....."
" Are you suffering from lung cancer? Have you smoked, or
worked in a factory where asbestos was used? You may be enti-
tled to a large sum of money. Call now...."

They become theatrical "performers." They self-promote, and not just locally. They like to fly in private jets and often dress differently than you and I. Two of these gentlemen always wear big Stetson cowboy hats and high-heeled cowboy boots, even though they live in the city and the boots and hats serve no purpose other than to make them seem taller. They are the "rhinestone cowboys" of the law.

Dennis Phillips was a local celebrity. There was hardly a television panel or radio show that discussed pending criminal cases that didn't include Dennis. He was the champion of the underdog. You remember the case, the Ricky Sapporter case, where the young defendant killed his parents. Dennis came up with the defense of "television intoxication." While the case was in the courts Dennis appeared on radio shows, television newscasts and gave interviews and was featured in the local newspapers. He gave speeches wherever he could be heard about the validity of his new criminal defense theory. "Television Intoxication." ..."Too much T.V. watching equals mental imbalance equals insanity." If one watches too much T.V. violence one becomes intoxicated by it and is no longer responsible for otherwise criminal behavior. He created his own pseudo-science along with the hack experts to get it heard in court. The jury convicted his client, but Dennis was famous.

Then there was Dennis' "Twinky" defense. Eat too many Twinkys, those delicious chocolate cakes, and you became insane and not responsible for your acts. "Sugar psychosis." The jury convicted again, but Dennis became even better known, nationally known.

* * * * *

I defended an automobile accident case in which Dennis was the plaintiff's attorney. He had an associate appear at the pretrial depositions, motions and conference. He would make his grand appearance at the trial. I had a pretty strong liability defense. His client had turned left immediately in front of our car. Even though the front of our car struck the side door of their car, we had no time to stop. They failed to yield the right of way. They claimed that we were speeding and could easily have avoided the collision and certainly contributed to it. The injuries were not severe. The day of the trial arrived. I had taken our client driver down to the courthouse for two dress rehearsals in a real courtroom, which had been vacant. He was placed in the real witness box and questioned and then cross-examined by me. On the second occasion he was grilled by my associate. I repeated this rehearsal three times. We cross-examined him about the skid marks, the location of the debris and the extent of the physical damages. He was asked to estimate the time that expired between the point at which he first noticed the other vehicle until the point of contact.

He marked the point of collision on a diagram of the intersection. He gave estimations of his own speed as well as the speed of the other car. This testimony was consistent with the accident report and the distances traveled by each vehicle after the impact. He could identify the other car and describe it. He could point out the other driver and he knew what he had been wearing. He knew what to expect. His testimony was consistent and dovetailed with our reconstruction expert. He knew to listen to the question and understand what was being asked before rushing to answer. That gives us time to object.

"We are not playing 'Beat The Clock'. Count to three before answering."

"Listen to our objections. We are guiding you."

We practiced that, too, and also practiced handling questions from out of the ballpark like "You admitted causing the accident to the police officer at the scene didn't you?"

The main thought was: "Don't rush to answer. Again, we are not playing 'Beat the Clock.' Give us a chance to object."

Our primary defense was that the other car pulled in front of us before we could stop or avoid it. We were ready. We met in our office in the morning, two hours before the time set for trial. The client was ready. We were ready. Our experts were on telephone call. Our team went down to the courthouse. Our associate, our trial secretary and the client were with me. We walked with confidence to the table marked "defense" on the left side of the courtroom, beyond the banister, and opened our briefcases and put our files and yellow pads on the table. It was five minutes to nine. No Dennis Phillips. The proper courtesy is to call opposing counsel's office to find out what was happening. At ten after nine there was no answer. We tried again at nine fifteen, and then at nine thirty I was called into the judge's office.

"How are you, Mr. Ress?"

"Just fine, Your Honor, but I can't find Mr. Phillips."

"You won't. He won't appear. Draw an Order of Dismissal with Prejudice."

"But he may be able to explain and would be entitled to re-file."

"Draw an Order Dismissing with Prejudice. Close your file. You'll never hear from him again."

The judge was right. The last I saw of Dennis was in a ten-kilometer footrace.

He waved to me.

Sandy Simon was the number one trial lawyer in Southeast Florida. He was wild in court. I don't think he, himself, could tell right from wrong and he didn't care. He would yell and scream, rant and rave and conduct a theatrical performance and he got away with it. The judges generally left him alone. He donated and raised large sums for their election and re-election campaigns and served on their committees. He knew all of the County Commissioners, State Senators and the Governor. He had a stable of medical specialists including professors, lecturers and traveling professional witnesses. His reconstruction experts were very creative. He used visual aids, huge graphic blow-up photographs, which other attorneys couldn't get past the judge, and expensive medical exhibits. His trial-experienced accountants could come up with huge sums for economic damages. He sued large corporations, insurance companies and hospitals for vehicle collisions, product liability and malpractice, often in class actions and always looking for punitive damages He brought in jury-evaluation experts who would get the list of proposed jurors in advance and research their backgrounds. As the jurors were being interviewed by the attorneys, they would watch for facial expressions and body language and guide you as to whether the juror would be sympathetic. He brought in huge verdicts.

As Sandy made more and more money, he built his own building with a recreated courtroom, complete with a high ceiling, State and U.S. flags, a raised platform for the judge, a witness stand and a jury box. Actually it was just like the real courtroom. He would put the clients on the stand and conduct entire mock trials, often having assistants bring in paid jurors from the street. Sandy tried the case two or three times before they went into the real courtroom. His team evaluated the practice jurors' comments and adjusted their presentation of the case. There is a great benefit from rehearsals, as any musician or anyone in show business will tell you.

The Aetna Casualty Insurance Company asked me to defend one of Sandy's cases. He screamed and yelled and coached during the depositions. The case involved a death at the Gulfstream racetrack. The manager of the track caterer was found beaten to death in the storeroom. Although there wasn't enough for a criminal charge and no one knew who did it, Sandy was suing the racetrack because they were the owners of the property, based on inadequate security. The attack had come during normal business hours. Security really wasn't an issue. Inadequate locks or lighting didn't have anything to do with this assault. The judge was friendly to Sandy and denied our Motion for Summary Judgment, allowing the case to go to trial before a jury. It appeared to me that we could win this case and should and would win this case. My reports went to the adjuster and supervisor at the Aetna. This case should be tried! On the eve of the trial I was "called off."

The case was settled for some crazy high amount. Oh, the benefit of publicity!

Sandy was one of the Florida lawyers who were asked to represent the State against the tobacco companies. Why? Because he was a famous "superlawyer." The attorneys representing the State of Florida received millions of dollars in attorneys' fees.

So I decided to send a case to Sandy that I thought could be won and the damages were significant. We were quite busy at the time and I wanted to see how Sandy would perform. After the case had dragged on for a long time. I received a letter, not a phone call. He had lost the case.

By the way, Sandy had to start his Rolls Royce with a remote control. He's made a few enemies along the way, and he didn't want to be sitting in the driver's seat if a bomb went off.

So much for superlawyers. I'm just a mediocrity. Sorry, dad.

15

Last Words

There were all kinds of accident cases running through our office. One of the most unusual ones involved four teenagers on Miami Beach who went out one night to have some thrills "skiing" with a Chevy Corsair. That's the little car with the motor in the back. We represented two of the passengers, young high-school girls, Gloria and Alice Berman. One wound up with a fractured pelvis and the other with plastic surgery and a small scar on her arm.

One of the man-made islands on the bay side of Miami Beach had a long straightway. At the end of about a quarter of a mile there was a "hump" bridge after which there was a sharp left turn, almost a "U" turn. The sport was to drive down the straightway as fast as the car would go, run up the bridge and fly into the air, ski-jumping the car and then landing and recovering in time to make the left turn. The crash occurred at about ten o'clock at night. The car jumped the bridge, but failed to negotiate the turn and slammed into a telephone pole on the side of the road. The car hit sideways and was almost split in two. The driver, John Fein, was the sixteen-year-old son of a prominent Miami Beach attorney. The young man in the right front seat, Paul Austin, died at the scene. His family had selected a flamboyant plaintiff's attorney to represent them, "T.J." Rance. (You bet I changed the name.)

The defense was that the passengers knew just what they were doing. They consented to it. They knew the risks of jumping the bridge and assumed them. They knew about the sharp left turn. They had all equally and willingly participated. They couldn't now complain that the driver was negligent. They admitted that they had done this before, although successfully and with a different driver.

The case involving the estate of Paul Austin, the young man who died, was called to trial first. I had filed a separate lawsuit for Gloria and Alice. My clients, the girls' parents, were very anxious to get their cases settled. They had medical and hospital bills with portions not covered by insurance. They didn't want their daughters to go through the tension of a trial. Both cases were being defended by the senior partner of a large defense firm located on an entire floor in a high-rise office building just next to the courthouse, namely Otis Walter. He was a tough, lanky, laconic, nasty, sourpuss and to make matters worse the driver's father had brought in Murray Smith, the famous plaintiff's trial lawyer, who was now also aggressively defending the young driver.

Nobody would even talk to me. I knew that if "T.J." won his case I would probably be able to settle mine. If we could help him it would help us and I had an idea.

"T.J." Rance was a known alcoholic and a wife beater. He agreed to speak to me at his office, but he only had a few minutes. He was stocky, blue-grey eyes, had sort of longish dirty blond hair and was wearing a light tan suit with a striped tie and a white shirt with cufflinks. He didn't look at me while I attempted to talk. In fact, before I could open my mouth he told me that he didn't need my suggestions and didn't want me telling him how to try the case. He had tried hundreds of cases like this and who was I to suggest how the case should be tried. He rose and escorted me to the door.

Otis Walter had me walking behind him from the courthouse down Flagler Street towards his office. The faster I walked to keep up with him, the faster this six-foot-four beanstalk of a man walked to keep me behind. He was snarling and very abruptly told me that there was no reason for them to settle and that they weren't offering one penny. He would see me in court. I was convinced that he and his firm represented the Ku Klux Klan. Murray Smith wouldn't take my calls even though I knew him from my first days in Miami and had interviewed for a job with him.

"T.J." didn't even nod to me at the courthouse. He tried a nondescript case. He showed blow-ups of the car and the crash scene. He put on an expert to testify as to the speed of the car before it went over the bridge. He argued that the car went out of control because of the negligence of the driver. He brought in the County Medical Examiner and established the cause and time of death and talked about his client's pain and suffering, since Paul died about a half hour after the accident. Otis Walker, in his grey three-piece suit, strode arrogantly in front of the jury and pounced on "T.J.'"s experts and picked away at his case. My girls were called to testify that they all had agreed to jump the bridge, knew it was dangerous and had done it before. After that, the cocky driver, John Fein, testified about the conversation before they

76

went out to jump the bridge, namely that they all agreed to do it. The jury was out for less than an hour. "We find for the defendant."

Now there was no hope for any settlement. My clients' father, Mr. Berman, was concerned about the costs of trial including witness fees due to the doctors and our accident reconstruction expert. We would have a new jury, but the same witnesses would testify. Especially damaging was the Fein boy who had been very carefully coached by Otis Walter and Murray Smith. There was an air of smugness to this kid and he didn't seem at all concerned that he had killed one young man and wounded two nice young girls. Not at all.

We had no choice. I told Mr. Berman that if we lost he would never see a medical or other expert witness bill so he had very little at risk.

Mr. and Mrs. Austin were in the back of the courtroom. They had learned that their son had some last words with one of my young girls and they asked if I would tell them what they were. I didn't know, but would find out.

We picked a jury and, as you may know, the case is often tried by making statements and designing questions to the proposed jurors that really explain your case and influence the jury. Some of my questions concerned whether each juror had a valid unrestricted driver's license. One of the jurors was a pilot, and I asked him to describe the necessary training and required experience before one was allowed to fly a passenger plane, particularly at night.

Our case pretty much paralleled the Austin trial. The reconstruction expert testified as to the way the accident happened, how the car skidded and the impact. I asked why there was no accident when cars had jumped the bridge in the past. The answer was that it would depend on the speed and the capability and experience of the other drivers. It was allowed in "for what it might be worth" said the judge. Of course the doctors testified and the hospital records and bill were introduced into evidence.

Then I called the Fein boy as an adverse party witness.

"Mr. Fein, at your deposition you showed me your driver's license. I show you a blow-up of it now. Please explain the word 'RESTRICTED' which appears in capitals at the bottom."

"I am not allowed to drive at night."

"But this accident happened after dark, at night. At around ten p.m. Right?"

"This was the only time I ever drove at night. I believe in following the law."

"Did you tell my girls Gloria and Alice that you had a restricted driver's license?"

"No."

"No further questions."

Fast forward to the final argument. The plaintiff gets to speak first and then again after the defendant's argument. When I got up to speak last I pretended to hold a microphone. I looked right at the jury.

"Ladies and gentlemen, this is your captain speaking. It's ten o'clock in the evening. We are on the ground at Miami International Airport about to take off for New York. We will be flying at thirty thousand feet. Oh yes! I forgot to tell you that I'm not allowed to fly this plane at night and I have never flown an airplane at night before. Would you like to get off?"

Otis Walters put his head down with his face in his hands. Smith was looking at the floor.

"Well Gloria and Alice were never given the opportunity to get off. To get out of that car with a driver who never told them that he wasn't allowed to drive at night and had absolutely no experience driving at night."

The jury was out quite a long time. I went across the street to Sally Russell's bar for a vodka. It took the jury five hours.

"We find for the plaintiffs and award damages of $300,000.00 to Gloria Berman and $75,000.00 to Alice Berman. So say we all."

The girls were hugging me. Mr. and Mrs. Austin had pushed their way up to me. By this time I had asked Gloria what those last words of Paul's were. I knew it was coming.

"Mr. Ress we're so excited and pleased for the Bermans. Mr. Ress could you please tell us what our son's last words were."

I couldn't get myself to sidestep or lie.

"They were: 'I can't believe that this is happening to me.'"

16

Striking Out

1. Dry Cleaning II

Mrs. Feiner was the wife of a well-known orthodontist. I had represented them when they built their home. She would march through the construction site daily nit-picking the contractor into oblivion. Dr. Feiner and his brother were pretty laid back and everyone liked him. He was charming, good-looking, very athletic, an excellent basketball player and a tournament tennis star. She was short, wiry and tough. She reminded me of Nancy Reagan and Pat Nixon combined. She had a mean squinty look in her eyes, a scowl on her face and looked as though she just swallowed a piece of lemon against her will. She continually asked me to take the contractor to task for insignificant things such as "the windows are dirty and one is cracked" or "there's dust on the floor." "Lady, it's a construction job." Finally it became distasteful to keep finding the most minor faults, which always exist in construction work. The builder was at the end of his rope and thinking of abandoning the job. So I wasn't surprised when she asked me to represent her in a dry cleaning case. I did have some experience representing dry cleaners and I had taken a course with the American Dry Cleaning Association

Mrs. Feiner dropped her dress off at the cleaners. It was a blue silk calf-length dress. The dress came back a mess. The chemicals damaged the fabric and the material was shredding. It was a three-hundred dollar dress and she wanted action.

When I told her that she could not sue for the matching gloves, belt, hat and shoes, she discharged me.

2. Too Good To Be True

What a case! Blind in one eye as a result of striking the dashboard in a rear-end collision. Mrs. Cantor, the driver, was unconscious at the scene. She complained of difficulty seeing, particularly her left eye. The doctors all agreed that based on the history of excellent vision before the accident and the immediate loss of vision afterward, the detached retina was caused by the trauma.

The insurance company wouldn't tender the policy limits of the responsible driver who ran into Mrs. Cantor. Not only that, there wasn't even an offer. A lawsuit was filed and discovery taken. The liability was clear. Still no offers.

We went to trial. A piece of cake, I thought. Everything went well. Our doctors all testified that she was legally blind in the left eye due to a detached retina, which by history was caused by the trauma of the accident. She had never had difficulty seeing before. She never even wore reading glasses. I was ready to give a great emotional plea for justice and a very large verdict. What would happen if she damaged the right eye? She was vulnerable.

Mrs. Cantor was the last of my witnesses and I turned her

over for cross-examination.

"Mrs. Cantor, you came from Philadelphia do you not?"

It was the defense counsel striding back and forth in front of the jury. A cocky guy considering the trouncing he had been receiving.

"Now you tell us under oath that you had perfect vision before this accident, right?

"Yes."

His eyes began to glow. His pace increased. He was addressing the jury with his questions, making eye contact with them and only glancing at my client.

"And you never had a problem with your left eye before, correct?

"Yes."

He was salivating as if he was going to devour her.

"Is this your social security number and your former Pennsylvania address on this document?"

It was a patient information card. In those days you could bring in documents as "rebuttal" without having to disclose them before the trial in the discovery procedure. She agreed that it was her social security number and former address.

He was now agitated, red in the face and almost shouting.

"This medical record from fifteen years ago reads, referring to you Mrs. Cantor, 'She comes in today for final discharge having suffered a detached retina of the left eye as a result of being struck by a golf ball three months ago."

Strike three! The doctors felt sorry for me and reduced their expert witness fees. I never saw or heard from Mrs. Cantor again.

3. Surprise!

Another automobile collision with good liability. This time Charley Perlman came to me after his chiropractor had run up ten thousand dollars in medical bills for highly questionable treatment. Charley was retired, likeable, tall, thin and a happy sort of fellow who always told the oldest and worst jokes, but you sort of had to like him. His wife Hilda, was also quite pleasant, always smiling and the kind of person who makes one feel that she is just glad to be alive.

Frankly, it wasn't the kind of case that I would ordinarily undertake. He had no objective evidence of any significant injury. His complaints of back pain, radiating down the leg with numbness in his toes, particularly his left leg and left foot, were consistent with a bulging or herniated lumbar disc. The x-rays showed some narrowing of the L5-S1 segment of the spine. (There were no MRI's in those days.) Our orthopedic surgeon found low-back muscle spasm. There was some limit of his ability to lift his left leg straight up in the air, about thirty percent limit.

The orthopedist tried some physical therapy and discharged Charley with a five-to-ten percent disability of the body as a whole based on his spasm and narrowing of the disc space, but primarily based upon his subjective limitations, limited by the onset of pain. The doctor opined that Charley should not sit or stand or single position himself for over one hour, was unable to repetitively bend, could not twist or lift anything over ten pounds. Charley's retirement activities of bowling and golf were over forever.

At his deposition where we could ask questions with a court reporter present, the defendant's orthopedic specialist said that at the "independent medical examination" he conducted he watched Charley come out of his car and walk into the office without any sign of injury or disability and when he left the office he observed him getting into his car without any hesitation, opening the door, hopping in and driving off. He observed Charley taking off and putting on his shoes while bending over, without any restriction, yet when he conducted a physical examination Charley was restricted and complained of pain while performing these same motions. At trial the doctor would have to admit getting quite a bit of business from the defense attorney and testifying for him regularly and being a hired snoop.

I thought that the case had some value, but it really was a case to settle. There was no mediation and we went to trial without any substantial offer being made. That alone should have told me something, but I saw only the believability of my clients as the issue and they were charming.

All of my clients receive a letter from me right at the beginning, and one of the items of concern is the possibility that you may be followed and movies taken of your activities. "Sometimes, on a good day we try to do some activities that we know better than to attempt, like changing a tire after the surveillance company had flatted it. Investigators lie in wait hoping that you'll remove the cement block which they placed in your driveway."

Usually the client brings on his or her own problem and denies engaging in that particular activity at their sworn pretrial deposition.

The Perlmans swore that they hadn't mowed their lawn and

had hired a lawn service at quite an expense. Charley hadn't bowled and left the senior league. As for golf, the clubs remained in the garage gathering dust. There were no independent intervening accidents.

Under the pretrial rules the defendant had to disclose surveillance films and they sure did. There was Charley bending over effortlessly to place the golf ball on the tee, swinging at the golf ball with his driver just like a pro. No hesitation, full backswing. There was Charley picking up the golf bag, slinging it over his shoulder and marching down the fairway. Wait a minute. I don't believe it. Here's Charley jumping over a creek while carrying his golf bag. The bag must weigh over thirty pounds.

Charley had denied playing golf.

4. That Doggie

"That doggie bit me."

The family sat in front of me telling me how their ten-year-old son won the National Baptist Outstanding Youth Award. It was a great honor. He was a national hero. Ben and his six-year-old brother, Todd, were at a neighbor's apartment and the kids were playing.

They were in a courtyard of the apartment complex and Todd went up to pet this fifty-pound German Shepherd, which was next to the wall on a long chain. Without warning the dog bared its teeth and started after Todd who was screaming. Ben went to the rescue and as he was pulling Todd away from the snarling animal the German Shepherd sunk its teeth into Ben's face. It took over fifty-five stitches and left a long irregular scar down the entire side of Ben's cheek. The scar was permanent.

Both parents, Mat and Mary Bolten, were quite proud of their son Ben. Ben had been awarded a medal and a trophy, which they showed me. A big silver oval suspended on a red, white and blue ribbon with a large cross on the top. The trophy bore the words:

"Hero of the Year, 1990
For Valor
The Baptist Council of the United States."

Impressive. The father was a painter with a small independent company and the mother was a secretary employed by the Baptist Church. She was plump, in her thirties and smiled a lot. She wore colorful long-sleeved cotton dresses with a silver crucifix displayed outside and low-heeled shoes. He was sort of drab, grey cotton pants and a brown polo shirt with brown boots. He wanted to know what the case was worth and who would control the money. It's not uncommon for people to want an evaluation of their case in terms of a financial recovery. Some even seek to borrow against it. I don't make promises.

Ben could describe the incident like a motion picture producer.

"We had to go past that doggie to get to the doorway. That doggie went after Todd. I pulled Todd away before that doggie could get him, but that doggie bit me and it hurt."

The boys had just entered a courtyard and were trying to get to their friend's door. They had done nothing to provoke the dog. Neither of them had any history of misbehavior. Both were average students. The dog had no history of biting any one, but it looked like a mean son of a bitch and in dog-bite cases there is a presumption of liability.

I guess I went over the scenario about thirty times with young Ben, whom I had gotten to know and like. He was a sweet kid. He parted his off-blond hair down the middle and was a round-faced happy fellow. His brother was too young to testify since he really had no concept of taking an oath to tell the truth.

My plastic surgeon expert witness said that he didn't have an eraser at the end of his scalpel and that a dermabrasion, grinding down the scar, might help when the scar became more mature, but that Ben would have a scar on his face visible at conversational distance for the rest of his life.

My good friend Ray Pearson, the former Circuit Judge, was on the other side of the case. The Philadelphia Insurance Company had the policy and they told me that my demand was so high, thanks to Mr. Bolten's insistence, they wouldn't even make an offer.

The case went to trial. I remember cross-examining their plastic surgeon, who had testified that scars were not necessarily unsightly or bad and that many cultures thought that they were attractive.

"As you know the Germans value dueling scars, especially saber scars on the cheek. They regard these as a sign of manliness."

"The South Pacific islanders, especially the Maori in New Zealand tattoo scars on their faces as a sign of beauty."

"In Africa and in Alaska native tribes persons effect facial scars as a sign of respect for their culture."

* * * * *

My turn.

"Doc, do we live here in America? Now in 1991? Ben isn't living with a tribe in Africa is he?"

"Doc. You're testifying here today as a board-certified plastic surgeon here in America in 1991 with Ben, right?"

"Didn't you train for many years to learn how to reduce scars? Did you do any training to learn how to put ON scars?"

"Doc, how long are you practicing here? Over twenty years. At any time did any patient ever in your entire practice come to you to have you put a scar on their face?"

"Doc, did you ever, ever RECOMMEND to any patient that they put a scar on their face?"

"Doc, did you ever professionally in your entire practice intentionally put a scar on anybody?"

"Doc, in fact you charge substantial fees to REDUCE scars, and to remove moles and skin blemishes throughout your entire practice... to make people look nice and acceptable and clean-faced and scar-free in OUR society. Right?"

We were doing great after the first day and Ray Pearson said that he would call Philadelphia and see if could get a reasonable offer. Mr. Bolten's eyes were shining. I learned long ago not to celebrate until the check clears the bank, and by that time the excitement is over.

It was time for Ben to testify. I had gone over his testimony until we all knew it by heart. His mother had heard it even more than I, at the hearings of the Baptist Church, at the award ceremony, at the hospital, at the doctor's offices, ad nauseam.

So on to the witness stand goes little Ben. He's wearing a

nice white shirt, slacks, black shoes, hair slicked down and parted in the middle. Good boy!

We go through the story for the one-hundredth time. No problem.

"...and then that doggie bit me. It hurt."

"Your witness."

Ray Pearson stands up. He approaches the witness stand. He is about six foot six and three hundred pounds, but to Ben he looked twelve-feet tall. A giant! His voice was deep and rumbled as though God was booming at Ben.

"Now Ben, tell us what REALLY happened."

"We were throwing rocks at that dog and it bit me."

Court adjourned.

* * * * *

Ray was always kind to me. We went back to his office and he called Philadelphia, not telling them what had happened, and got a very reasonable settlement for me.

The next day the judge approved the settlement and discharged the jury. We were allowed to speak to the jurors and I asked the elderly Jewish grandfather, the juror who I had singled out to sway, what he thought of the case.

"I wouldn't have given that kid one red cent."

17

Say It Isn't So

The Naturopath

Florida was always a "right to work" State. That means that it was anti-union. You cannot compel a worker to join a union even though the majority of his working "brothers" are union persons. No "collective bargaining." An employee can be fired without "cause." Nevertheless the unions were pretty powerful. All of the unions were deeply concerned about workers' compensation benefits and offered to represent union members in comp cases without charge. Of course they didn't tell the workers that if they obtained any benefit, any benefit at all under the law, attorneys' fees were paid by the employers' insurance company. To be a union comp attorney could mean early retirement.

Eli Susskin was a loud, bumptious, bald, overweight plaintiff's union lawyer with more business than he and his partner, Joe Kappy, could handle. They were "volume" lawyers and you could settle many of the small cases with them under a secret, but well-known formula. Pay the physical disability "rating" (their doctor's numerical rating, usually five or ten percent, times five hundred dollars per point which would total between $2,500.00

to $5,000.00) plus an attorney's fee of about $1,500.00 and the case was over. No more medical payments. No ability to modify the claim to seek more benefits in the future. Close your file. For them it was like fifty cases a week. They undoubtedly greased the palm of the referring union officials, but who cared? The insurance companies were glad to clear out the cases at very reasonable prices. The workers got money fast. The unions looked good. Eli and Joe were making big bucks and the Florida Workers' Compensation Bureau was moving cases along and the statistics looked great.

Eli kept stretching his influence and power. Eli's brother-in-law Irvin Marcus was a naturopath. They were licensed professionals of God knows what, in Florida. They could have you eat pancakes to increase your virility and charge for doing so. They could bill insurance companies for what was very possibly quackery and they certainly took advantage of it.

Eli kept wondering why my client didn't invoke the formula and settle a rather open and shut case with him. It went to hearing. He clearly had referred in his brother-in-law who had billed out about four thousand dollars in highly questionable heat treatment, electrical massage, manipulations, herbal cocktails, inhalation therapy and vitamin consultations. These treatments were over a four-month period during February, March, April and May and were just about daily.

Irvin Markus, D.N. (Doctor of Naturopathy) testified under oath, with a court reporter transcribing, that he himself administered each of these treatments and they were performed, each of them, in his downtown Miami office, and in the presence of his nurse, who was his wife, and that she was prepared to so testify.

He described each treatment, how it was performed and how long it lasted. He testified to the accuracy of the bills that he sent out and that the dates and times were all correct and that he had collected the four thousand dollars in treatment charges. At the end of the cross-examination I confronted him with the hospital records showing that the very same person he claimed he was treating in his office was actually a full time in-patient at the hospital for over a month in February and March for an unrelated disease while Irvin was billing daily for treatments. Over twenty treatments were totally fraudulent and fictitious. He turned red, then white. He wriggled in his chair and his brother-in-law tried to rescue him.

"Irvin, don't say anything more. We invoke the Fifth Amendment. My client was entrapped."

"First of all, Mr. Susskin, you represent the injured worker and have a conflict of interest since he also was defrauded and his case damaged by your brother-in-law. I am requesting the Judge of Compensation Claims to refer this matter to the State's Attorney's Office for Criminal Investigation."

The workers' compensation Judge now squirmed in his seat. They know better than to get involved in any criminal prosecution or to "make waves." All he was truly interested in was retirement on government pension checks plus Social Security.

"Judge, I think we might resolve this matter with the following agreement. Mr. Markus returns the naturopathic fees he obtained. We settle the claim per the usual formula since the client shouldn't have to suffer because of Eli's brother-in-law—and finally that Irvin Markus agrees never to treat or ever testify again in a workers' compensation case."

I never saw or heard from Irvin Marcus again.

My Doctors Aren't That Much Better

My dear friend Kenny, the one-eyed brain surgeon with the enormous I.Q., was the treating doctor in a crane accident case that I was unable to get settled. We showed up in court at nine in the morning on a bleak Monday. It was dark and cold even for Miami. My client was a gentle middle-aged, middle-everything. Mid-level corporate employee. Mid-sized. Mid-level intelligence. Mid-economic level. Average everything. Married. Two kids. Nice quiet wife. Nice house. Nice car. Nice guy.

When we arrived in the courthouse I visited with the opposing attorney and the insurance adjuster. The defense attorney, as usual, was a pain in the butt, boasting about how he is going to win the case and that we have no chance of success, all in front of his client. Privately John Thomas wants to get a few days of billing in, but Court time is easily traceable and you can't get twenty hours of billing in an eight-hour court appearance. You can charge for preparation, meeting with witnesses and clients, review of reports and records, research, but there are only twenty-four hours in each day and clients start to realize that billable hours are being manufactured. So once the trial gets started and the hours can easily be tracked, the attorneys have an economic interest in settlement. It's nice to be able to pay the bills.

I put out a settlement number to the adjuster. We need another one hundred thousand dollars to get it done. He says that it's beyond his authority. He's in a tight spot. No matter what the case settles for, a supervisor who comes in periodically from the home office will review the file and say that they paid too much. While if the case is tried, no matter how bad the result, you can always blame the crazy jurors in Miami or the corrupt court system. The claims adjuster that settles too many cases is signing a death warrant on his longevity with some companies.

The adjuster and the claims manager in the insurance company's local office had put a "reserve" value on the file. This was reviewed periodically and adjusted. There are a number of reasons for this, including government insurance regulations requiring the insurance carrier to keep adequate cash reserves. The object of the adjuster now is to bring the case to a conclusion within the reserve.

The local adjuster's individual authority to settle is generally quite low and meant to move out nuisance cases. Even the local claims manager has little settlement authority. Maybe at the time of this trial it was something like fifteen thousand dollars. The State manager probably would have fifty thousand in authority and the regional manager something like seventy-five thousand. Once you hit one hundred thousand dollars you are talking about committees in the home office and they don't meet every day. However, when there is a reserve on the case there may be a person watching the case at the home office with power to settle it without having to go through committee again.

The adjuster was nice enough.

"Lewis, I'll make some calls and see if I can't get the authority."

"That's all that I can ask. Thanks, Tom."

The Clerk calls the case and we both answer: " Ready."

The judge enters: "All rise…"

My client would like the case resolved mid-way between our demand and their offer. With him everything is "mid-way." We're one hundred thousand dollars apart and neither side is moving. The jury panel enters through a separate door. They are seated in the jury box, which has three tiers of chairs. Normally the judge starts off by asking the assembled group a set of standard questions.

" Have any of you served on a jury before?" – and on he goes with about ten questions.

Some judges limit the attorneys, but most of the time we are allowed to ask the jurors our own questions. It's called "voir dire." We are really looking for potential jurors' reactions, facial expressions, body language such as crossing their arms over their chest, tilting their head down, avoiding eye contact with us, and their willingness overall to answer candidly. We try to influence the jury and "sell" our case by asking suggestive questions.

"We are going to produce an expert who will tell us about the safety requirements in the operation of a large crane. Do any of you know how to operate a large crane? Will you agree to listen to the expert? Do you have respect for the opinions of experts? ....,"

If the case is big enough we might bring in a jury selection expert, usually a psychologist, who watches and listens and suggests who to challenge off the jury.

We can challenge for "cause," such as instances where the juror says that he or she does not believe in the jury system, or that they would never award any money to an injured plaintiff no matter what the circumstances. We can use our pre-emptive challenges—usually you get three—to remove anyone you believe might be tilted against your client for any reason, provided your challenge is not based on racial or religious bias.

We spend the rest of the morning and into the afternoon questioning the jury, trying to learn how they think. We start to tell them about the case and watch their individual reactions.

" As I have mentioned, this is a case about the operation and function of a large crane. Do any of you or members of your family have experience or training operating a crane? What about other construction equipment? Do you agree that large cranes require careful operation, with specialized training?"

Are they liberal, empathetic to injured people, sensitive, compassionate, Democrats or are they hard-nosed, tight-fisted, conservative Republicans.... or wackos of some sort? Have they or any of their family or close friends been in an accident, served on a jury, made or defended a claim? What happened? Where do they work? Where do they live? Alone? With family? What do they do? Accountant? (watch out) Laborer? (understands the working man). What are their hobbies? What organizations do they belong to? Do they or anyone in their family have presently or in the past suffered an injury or a disability? Are they or anyone in their family involved in the Court system, the claims business, the medical industry? How do they feel about awarding large sums when it is justified? Can and will you do it?

How are they dressed? Overdressed with tie, jacket, cufflinks, cordovan shoes? (Conservative). Underdressed in a sweatshirt, khakis, sneakers? (Liberal free-thinker).

Sometimes I have my investigator look at their cars which are parked in the special jurors' parking lot to see what make and model they drive, the color of the car and most importantly any bumper stickers. "America for Americans!" (That's telling you something.)ly

Even while the case is being tried it's a good idea to get all the information you can about the jurors, including credit reports.

Now, in the guise of asking questions, it is time to try your case in front of the prospective jurors.

"This is a case of a significant permanent injury arising from an admittedly dangerous operation of a large crane which fell over and struck my client Mr. Average. You are going to hear from a number of experts who will take the stand. Do any of you know Mr. Saltinstal, the mechanical engineer or Dr. Lustig the neurosurgeon?"

It goes on into the afternoon. The defense lawyer gets his licks in too.

"You don't believe in rewarding exaggerated claims do you? If you do, please raise your hands."

"You realize that you have a duty to screen out the truth from the money seeking fiction in this case. Do any of you question that?"

"You will hear that this plaintiff, Mr. Average, put himself in the wrong place at the wrong time. In other words, he positioned himself negligently and therefore cannot make a full recovery, but only a proportionate recovery. Will you agree to apply that rule if the Judge tells you about it from the bench?"

Objecting doesn't always help you when the jury is being questioned. They aren't dumb. They quickly figure out what is going on. They listen to what you are saying and expect you to prove it during the trial. The judge often tends to other business on the raised bench where you can't see what he or she is reading.

The jury selection process goes into the second day. At long last the jury is selected and alternates are also seated. The remainder of the potential juror pool is sent back to the jury assignment room for possible service in other cases, or allowed to go home.

We pass by one another again before trial starts and the insurance adjuster says that he hasn't heard anything back, but increases the offer by twenty thousand. We are now eighty thousand dollars apart. He also is no dope. I say that I will meet with my client and suggest resolving the matter for an additional sixty thousand. My client says:

"Why don't we just take the additional twenty thousand and be done with it?"

"Hang on," says I. "There'll be more coming. Just be patient. Sometimes these cases get settled while the jury is out deliberating. Let's see how the case goes."

If things go right I am planning on asking the jury for a million dollars.

The actual trial starts. Both attorneys think that they have good jurors who will rule with them. Each attorney singles out one or two of the six to "play" to. That is, to address with the eyes, and with statements designed to appeal to certain of their beliefs.

The judge addresses the jury. He cautions them not to discuss the case amongst themselves until both sides rest and they retire to the jury room to deliberate. One juror has a question. Yes, they may make notes. They are sworn in by the clerk of the court.

Here we go.

Opening Statements:

"Ladies and Gentlemen of the jury, my name is Lewis Ress and I represent Mr. Average sitting right here who was badly injured when the American Construction Company's crane, operated by Charles Evans, sitting right over there, whose training or lack of it as you will hear about, was the cause of this accident. This crane was so negligently and improperly positioned and secured that it toppled and fell in a wind that was well within the range of "expected events" and caused Mr. Average to be severely injured, for life!

"You will hear from our experts as to the rules and regulations that American Construction violated...."

"Mr. Average was on the property in order to deliver a document to the construction office and was walking in an unrestricted area. Any claim that he positioned himself negligently is just nonsense and I am certain that you will see right through that defense...."

"That is the liability side of this case. We will prove that American Construction's negligence was the cause of Mr. Average's injuries...."

"You will hear the testimony of Dr. Kenneth Lustig a neurosurgeon, concerning the nature and extent of Mr. Average's injuries and the effect they have on his ability to work and to enjoy his personal life. He will have these restrictions and limitations for the rest of his life."

And I go on to describe what is going to happen. John Thomas objects a few times, but the judge allows that Mr. Thomas will have his own "time" with little or no interruption.

The case is going well. The engineer, Abe Saltinstal, was terrific. He described all the government safety rules and regulations. American had been cited before. We were on the edge of punitive damages. He nailed them.

"Mr. Thomas, one could easily conclude that the very fact that this accident happened is proof of negligence, since cranes don't fall unless they are not rigged or secured properly."

I was now ready for Dr. Lustig. He was due ten minutes before I intended to call him to the witness stand. Sometimes we even interrupt other witnesses in order to accommodate a doctor. I called his office. (There were no cell phones in those times.)

"Mr. Ress, He's on the way. He left over a half hour ago."

Dr. Lustig practiced in North Miami Beach, toward the north part of the county. It was a three-quarter hour trip to the courthouse and then there was parking.

I put Mr. Saltinstal back on the stand to kill some time and then I asked the judge for a half-hour recess. At the end of the recess I requested some additional time to allow for Dr. Lustig's travel. Suddenly the reality came upon me. Dr. Lustig was going to be a NO SHOW! He wasn't coming. I called his office again. They hadn't heard from him and didn't know where he was. Mr. Average's chart was on his desk!

I found John Thomas talking to the adjuster in an alcove.

"Gentlemen, I can stop Dr. Lustig and we won't have to pay his five thousand dollar witness fee. Let's add it into the pot and see if we can't get this case settled."

"Lewis, I can add five to match which would mean ten thousand more and that's it."

"Tom, the case is settled!"

Kenny Lustig and I were close friends right up until the day he died. I even put a pebble on his gravestone about twice a year.

He never told me why he just didn't show up. It was not a subject up for discussion.

Ever.

The Special Treatments

Dr. Arthur Gomez was a highly respected orthopedic specialist with an office in North Miami. The workers' comp insurance carriers were allowed to select the treating doctors and paid them when a claim was accepted as being compensable. The injured worker in this case was Zena, a middle-aged Hispanic woman who sprained her back in a lifting accident at work. She had been treated and was discharged by Dr. Gomez with a zero disability and with no restrictions. And no need for future care. The claimant's attorney paid for an "independent" medical exam with his own doctor who he used for this purpose on a regular basis. He said that Zena needed more treatment and would be left with a minimal permanent partial disability to the body as a whole. He based his testimony upon her consistent subjective complaints. Zena's case came up for hearing and Dr. Gomez assured me that:

"Ress, we were going to win this one."

I didn't know, nor did I guess what was coming. I cross-examined their doctor, Frank Steele, and he agreed that he could find no objective tangible evidence other than muscle spasm to support Zena's complaints, and that in assigning a permanent disability rating he primarily relied on her sincerity.

Dr. Arthur (Arturo) Gomez took the stand with a bit of a swagger. He went through his normal routine about all of the tests he performed and that her complaints were inconsistent and incompatible with a low-back injury. Then came the surprise.

"Mr. Ress, let me tell you why this lady is a crock. I injected her five separate times over five different weeks. She got immediate and complete relief with each injection, going through all of the tests, which she now complains of, without the slightest limitation or complaint. Then she said that the injection wore off and her back became painful again.

Well, Mr. Ress, those injections were purely saline solution, that is, water. She is a complete phony."

The judge bought it.

I explained to the insurance company that I didn't authorize the doctor to engage in unpermitted body assaults or trickery. I also was aware of the "placebo effect" where validly injured patients actually improve with non-effective treatments like sugar pills, but I had a duty to try my case, not my opponent's.

Another One of My Wild Doctors

The sixty-year-old white-haired wiry thin man hurt his back when he fell at work and he couldn't or wouldn't straighten up. He went around bent over at the waist. He was claiming lifetime permanent total disability. The plaintiff's doctors could not find the cause of the trouble, but he walked straight up before and now he was bent over. The plaintiff's psychiatrist said that his patient suffered from "bent back syndrome" and related it to the accident and testified that the injured worker would require palliative psychiatric treatment for the rest of his life and could not perform the duties of the easiest of jobs. Work again? Never.

We were looking at twenty years of psychiatric care, two sessions a week plus medication and weekly workers' compensation checks... maybe three million dollars.

Based on my experience with psychiatrists I realized that this was going to be another "battle of the doctors," which the insurance companies regularly lose. One good thing was that we could control who the treating doctors would be.

Benjamin Walters had originally been a dentist. He lost his right thumb in a woodworking accident on his bench saw at a time when one was unable to have it re-attached. So he was left with an unsightly stump and scars all over his hand. Ben's right hand was pretty much useless. It was the end of dentistry and the beginning of psychiatry. Ben was like his hand, short and stumpy and tough. After graduating with honors from the University of Miami Medical School, he entered a residency program and became a board-certified psychiatrist. He accepted workers' compensation cases and believed in aggressive treatment with no coddling.

I sent the bent back case over to Ben and waited. Ben called:

"Lewis, I saw your bent back case. I'll have the gentleman cured and back to work in two weeks."

I didn't believe that old wives' tale.... He probably was just bragging. We had over one million dollars in the reserves on this claim; but, sure enough, the very next week the claimant's attorney calls up and wants to settle, cheap.

I call Dr. Walters.

"Ben, Ben what did you do? I hear that the old man is walking straight as an arrow and wants his old job back. What did you do?"

"Lewis, this was a very simple case. I explained to the patient that I would be treating him for a long time, possibly for the rest of his life. I then gave him his first treatment where I greased up a cattle prod with plenty of Vaseline and stuck it up his ass and gave him a hellova jolt. He straightened up pronto. I gave him a second jolt just so he could get the idea embedded in his skull. I told him to make an appointment with Laura for next week for a treatment every day. He said that he was cured and didn't need any more treatments."

18

A Case I Wanted To Lose

The Miami Daily News was calling for a conference. One of their newsboys was seriously injured while hawking papers on the street. He had head injuries and a severely fractured hip. He might be paralyzed from the waist down. The issue was going to be whether or not he was an employee or an independent contractor.

"We have to defend this case vigorously. It is a matter of principle. Our very existence depends on our newsboys being independent contractors."

That was the general manager. A twelve-year-old child was an independent contractor? It was the first and only case I can remember wanting to lose.

Charley Sims was eleven years old when he learned from some of his friends that you could make money by delivering or selling newspapers. He was a skinny little African-American kid with a big grin. He had holes in the bottom of his tennis sneakers. His father had left the family when Charley was three and his mom worked as a maid. They lived with his grandparents in a wooden house in downtown Miami. Grandpa was a mailman, but got paid as a part-time worker. Grandma took in ironing. Between the three wage earners they barely got by.

The other kids took Charley to the corner where *The Miami Daily News* distributor would bring his truck to unload. Mr. Mick, the distributor, gave Charley a paper to have his mother sign. It said that she understood and agreed as Charley's parent that he would be an independent contractor for Mr. Mick and not an employee.

Charley would pick up newspapers at a place designated by *The Miami Daily News* distributor and sell them on a particular street corner selected by the distributor at a set time each day and would turn over the money he received, return the unsold papers and be paid by the distributor based on the number of papers he sold each week.

He would at all times follow the rules and regulations as set down by the distributor and would keep a strict account of the money he received from sales and would not be tardy. If he missed work he would be docked and if he missed too much time he would be terminated.

He could get a friend to be a substitute in an emergency, but not on a regular basis. He would have to attend newsboy meetings. He would behave in a respectful and refined manner. He would wear a collared shirt, have a haircut and be clean.

There was no room for discussion or negotiation with *The Miami Daily News* or the distributor.

Mrs. Sims didn't understand the three-page single-spaced contract, which was loaded with legal jargon. There were a lot of "whereas" clauses. Nevertheless she signed at the "x" mark, where it said "parent and/or guardian."

Mr. Mick drove Charley to his assigned street corner at Northwest 54th Street and 27th Avenue and showed him how to fold the newspaper and hold the paper up in the air and wave it slightly so that drivers could see it, but not read it.

"Stand up straight. Smile. Fold the paper in two. Like this. Then hold it up with your left hand and move it around. Keep smiling. Say 'Thank you sir or madam' when they buy. Use your right hand to handle the change."

It later came out that Mrs. Sims, who had a fifth-grade education, was under the impression that Mr. Mick, the distributor, was a representative of *The Miami Daily News*. In fact, Mr. Mick drove a big silver metallic truck that was titled in his own name, but fully financed and supplied by *The Miami Daily News*. Mick merely signed his name on a document and was given the keys to the truck. *The Miami Daily News* held a large lien on the title. All the distributors had the same type of Ford truck, all the same make and all the same model. Some even had *The Miami Daily News* name printed on the side, although they were instructed to keep the truck free of any signs.

The distributors were also required to attend meetings, follow rules and regulations, not use the truck for any other work or activity and could not carry passengers. They each were assigned a very specific exclusive district within *The Miami Daily News* service area.

They were not to distribute or sell in any other distributor's area. Mr. Mick bought his newspapers from the *News*. They set the price. There was no bargaining. Mick was told what the newsboys were to charge. Mick returned the unsold copies to the *News* and was given a credit. Mick's contract with the *News* also said that he was to be an "independent contractor", but the rules and regulations made both Mick and Charley goodwill ambassadors for *The Miami Daily News*.

And so *The Miami Daily News* had an army of over fifty distributors and hundreds of children, mostly black, from poor, uneducated families out working for them, out in the streets as sales persons in the newspaper's sales network, without any insurance or other protection.

It was a drizzly evening in February with the temperature hovering at around sixty-five degrees when the rusty old uninsured lawn service pick-up truck hit Charley as he was standing in the street, smiling, with his left hand up in the air showing *The Miami Daily News*. The ambulance took him, unconscious, to Jackson Memorial Hospital. He was uninsured and the family was billed for his concussion and his fractured hip, which didn't paralyze him, but would result in a foreshortened leg with a permanent limp. Mrs. Sims was a mess. She had trouble taking time off to visit Charley and then the bills started coming in for thousands and thousands of dollars with threats of lawsuits, collection company calls, and the destruction of what credit she had.

The Miami Daily News steadfastly denied any liability or responsibility for Charley. They took the position that he was an independent contractor of an independent contractor. I defended them when Ira Druber, a bright Harvard Law School graduate, took on Charley's case. Druber filed for workers' compensation benefits, claiming that Charley was an employee of an agent of *The Miami Daily News* and in effect an employee of *The Miami Daily News*, taking orders from and being controlled by them through Mr. Mick.

Druber contested the Independent Contractor agreement which Mrs. Sims signed as being against public policy, being replete with legal conclusions, not being fully explained to Mrs. Sims so that she could understand it, and allowing minors to be subject to great risks without being adequately represented or protected. He argued that in fact *The Miami Daily News* controlled the details of Charley's work which was being performed in furtherance of their business and which was an integral part of the newspaper business, and that the independent contractor defense was a sham. Charley was really an employee.

Druber showed that *The Miami Daily News* had a sales force. They controlled how the sales were made, where they were made and the price for the goods sold. Charley wasn't like a lawn man, who could take on as many or few lawns as he wished, set his own prices, control his own hours, who owned his own equipment and could hire others to do the work. Charley had to attend meetings. He was told exactly how he was to do his job. He had a specific street corner, exclusively. He paid the price the *News* had set and sold at the price the *News* set. This was a scheme to illegally and unethically exploit child labor and now Charley's life was damaged forever and his mother was bankrupt.

The Miami Daily News had a strong case, too. Newsboys were deemed independent contractors historically. The newspapers could not exist without a distribution network, and if the newsboys would become employees the child labor laws would prohibit their employment. Even if an exemption was obtained, the cost of paying them salaries with fringe benefits like social security and workers' compensation would be prohibitive, and the newspapers would lose circulation, lose advertising and probably go out of business because the public was not going to pay large amounts for the daily paper.

The Miami Daily News argued that the contract was binding, being signed by the parent and natural guardian of the child. *The Miami Daily News* didn't control Charley's duties or obligations to attend meetings or instruct him how to sell papers. The independent distributor had only made suggestions. *The Miami Daily News* had no control over the distributors. Newspapers were sold to the distributors who resold them to the newsboys and the newsboys resold them for a profit. Once Charley was selling papers he was acting alone. He could perform in accordance with his own methods and was responsible only for the results of his work.

The workers' compensation judge was a political appointee. The Governor was not about to undo the Florida Supreme Court's earlier ruling in favor of *The Miami Herald* and go to war with the state's major newspapers. Mrs. Sims signed the agreement and bound her son by doing so. Contracts must have meaning. This one was not clearly against public policy, but in fact served a public need to assure that a free press was able to reach the community at a fair price.

Claim dismissed. The claimant was not an employee.

Druber's appeal to the Florida Supreme Court was not well received. *The Miami Herald* newsboy case of 1956 governed. There was no need to overturn good law.

The Miami Daily News was started back in 1896 as *The Miami Metropolis*. It became *The Miami Daily News*, the local evening paper, in 1925. Later on it occupied a famous building on Biscayne Boulevard, which is now the "Freedom Tower" and was the processing center for Cuban refugees escaping Castro.

The *News* built its own new building on the Miami River, but faltered economically, and around 1973 moved in with the morning newspaper, *The Miami Herald. The Miami Daily News* died on December 31, 1988.

"The Law Must Be Stable and Yet Cannot Stand Still"

That was the gold-lettered maxim cut into the paneled wall in the Cornell Moot Courtroom. It's still there. I always wondered what it really meant. Evidently it means that there comes a time when the law gets outmoded and has to be changed, whether by a new statute or by more reasoned judicial decisions. In case you haven't noticed, there are no more newsboys selling papers on the streets. It took quite a while, but the law must have finally moved on.

Charley Sims is still limping around.

19

The Million-Dollar Fee

Million-dollar fees don't just happen every day.

It was a strange set of facts.

There was this Tiki bar down in the Keys. It was at Bud and Mary's Marina on the Atlantic side of the road in Marathon. The sign was a huge marlin hanging on a block and tackle. Maybe thirty fishing boats were docked at the marina, with their chrome tuna towers rising above the roof of the Tiki bar. A concrete pedestrian bridge led out onto a platform raised above the Atlantic by about ten feet. There were wooden columns, really large stained trees, supporting a frame roof covered with palm fronds. The open bar alone was big enough to serve over fifty people. Two bartenders worked rapidly with sleeves rolled up, shaking the rum Mai Tais. The drinks flowed.

The Millennium Advertising Company was having a big bash there. They owned and leased the billboards for almost half of the State of Florida. Big, big bucks. The Miami officers were partying along with the rest of the South Florida staff. Although there were piles of stone crab claws and iced shrimp, there was very little dining, but a great deal of boozing. It started at eleven in the morning and went on and on. Robert James, the corpulent, white-skinned, red-faced, slightly balding host who was wearing a red-flowered short-sleeved shirt, khaki shorts and Birkenstock sandals, had finished pumping hands and back patting and was ready to head back to Miami, except that he was bombed. He had consumed at least six Mai Tais, each loaded with three types of rum, and was wobbling when he got up from his barstool and had to be walked to his car and helped in. They were afraid to tell him not to drive. He was the Regional Manager. It was a good way to get fired.

He drove off heading up US 1 toward Miami, the black four-door Mercedes 550 swaying from one side of the lane to the other. How he made it as far as the Palmetto Expressway into the North Dade County area is amazing, but he managed. He was getting off the expressway and heading towards Miami Lakes when he veered over into the oncoming lane of traffic and slammed head on into a blue Ford. The Mercedes was doing about fifty miles an hour with the Ford going about thirty. The explosion could be heard for a half mile. The front end of the Ford was totally blown off and crushed into the body of the car

My client, Ernesto (Ernest) Roberto Gomez, had been heading home from work as a maintenance man at the Killian High School. Although he had a seat belt on, the airbag didn't fully deploy and his skull struck and shattered the windshield. A better description was that the windshield struck and shattered Ernest's skull. Robert James was drunk, his body loose, and he was only scratched.

Millennium's attorneys pleaded James "no contest," with a prearranged drunk driving suspended sentence and a five-hundred-dollar fine. It was good enough for me because the civil side of the case allowed a "no contest" plea to be interpreted as accepting responsibility for the accident. Anyhow, I was just as happy to show the photographs and prove the negligence. I was going to seek punitive damages which can be assessed when the defendant's behavior is willful, wanton and with utter disregard for the safety of others, and Millennium would face the same damage claim since they allowed and assisted Robert James to drive drunk. In addition the Tiki Bar was responsible. They had no assets or insurance and were on the brink of bankruptcy. They have since disappeared.

James and Millennium never sent a get-well card or flowers or even inquired as to Ernest's injuries or his recovery. I didn't like James, with his white face and red nose, nor did I like his arrogant, boozing, pompous company—which I found employed no blacks, Jews, women, other than in secretarial positions, or Hispanics.

Ernest had been taken to Palmetto General Hospital and the neurosurgeon on call, Dr. Ovita, inserted a three-by-two-inch kidney-shaped titanium plate into the upper left front part of his skull to fill the gap where the skull had been splintered. It was attached with metal staples. Ernest healed beautifully and his skull hardly showed the scar, which was just below the hairline and then went into the scalp area. It was visible, and there was a depression in the front of his skull, but the injury was not defacing.

Ernest was having other troubles. He had occasional dizzy spells with loss of balance. His vision was not as clear and couldn't be corrected. His memory was affected. His personality had changed. He was quiet, soft-spoken, hesitant. He lost his zest for life. His neck and upper back were painful. He used a cane, although none had been prescribed. He hadn't been able to work and the school had replaced him.

I met with Dr. Ovita, a short, balding, dark-complexioned, quiet man in his mid-fifties and paid him generously for the consult. He had been on call at the Palmetto General Hospital when Ernest arrived by ambulance. We talked in his small, poorly lit office. Dr. Ovita made eye contact and didn't blink. He was direct and a bit clipped, but he gradually and begrudgingly agreed that the dizziness, loss of balance, vision and memory problems were all related to the accident. It was like pulling teeth, but finally Dr. Ovita assigned a fifteen percent permanent partial disability and suggested psychiatric treatment. A few weeks later the psychiatrist, Dr. Pearl, said that Ernest would require ongoing supportive care and would have a ten percent disability from an emotional standpoint. They both concluded that Ernest would not be able to resume his old job.

Global Indemnity had written Millennium's basic automobile policy, which was for one million dollars. They wouldn't even talk to us. There was a five-million-dollar "excess" policy coverage with Glacier Insurance Group. We filed suit, and Global had Ernest evaluated by their team of doctors—in reality, professional witnesses. These professional prostitutes made a terrific second income just by testifying time after time for the insurance companies. They always say either that the injuries didn't come as a result of the accident, or that the injured party was faking his or her pain and disability. Everyone makes a full recovery without any residual disability and never needs further treatment. The

Court wouldn't allow you to ask how much money they made from the insurance company for whom they were testifying. It required too much expensive paperwork. It was no surprise that Global's brain specialist said that Ernest made a full recovery and had no disability.

Their psychiatrist said that Ernest was fine, but "should avoid the stress of a trial and should settle his case."

The family said that Ernest really was doing great, would like to go back to work and to please get his case resolved, but they agreed that they would leave the matter in our firm's hands. There was nothing to discuss. There were no settlement offers.

It is a multipurpose tactic. We prepared a thirty-page plastic-covered book, which was a cross-indexed outline of our case, starting with the clear liability. It included pictures of the damaged vehicles, copies of the accident report and the "no contest" drunk-driving plea and continued on with the list of medical and hospital and prescription bills, the medical diagnosis, the disability evaluations. Attached were positive prints of the x-rays, photos of our client's scars and an outline of his lost past and future income, plus the outline of the damages, including Ernest's physical limitations, his need for future medical care and its cost. In addition we spelled out the claim for pain and suffering and his wife's claim for loss of services. We attached the life expectancy tables, and the final page showed a computation and basis for a damage claim of three million dollars, which did not include the claim for punitive damages not covered under the insurance policy.

We sent a copy by certified mail to both Global and Millennium and told them that we would be willing to accept the basic policy insurance of one million dollars as settlement and would waive the punitive damage claim if they agreed to settle. We set five p.m. on a Friday afternoon one month ahead as a deadline. It was a set-up for a "bad faith" claim against Global. If Global could settle within their policy limits and they unreasonably failed to do so it would expose them for whatever a jury awarded, even though there was another excess insurance company. We expected Millennium to pressure Global to settle and, if Global failed to do so, to sue Global for "bad faith" should the recovery exceed one million dollars.

After Global received the outline we called them and wrote to them weekly to remind them of the deadline... No response. Finally the fateful Friday arrived. I sat at the phone waiting and hoping and waiting and hoping some more... It was a nervous wait. The phone never rang. No offer whatsoever. So be it. It was war!

We started taking sworn statements, as did Global. It was our doctors against their doctors. I was surprised that Global's attorneys did not dig very deep. They sent out young associates to take the depositions and they generally followed a written prepared list of standard questions. They failed to ask if our doctors had any photographs.

Their doctors both said that Ernest could work without any limitation and had no disability and needed no further treatment. However, their psychiatrist, Dr. Bianco, again warned:

"Mr. Gomez should avoid the stress of a trial. It would be very damaging to him from an emotional point of view. He should settle his case as soon as possible."

I was in Dr. Ovita's office. Dr. Ovita asked me to stay for a few minutes after Global's attorneys were finished with his deposition.

"Mr. Ress, I have taken a liking to you and I know that you are trying to help Gomez and that it's not just the money, but you're dedicated. Also you have been a gentleman with me. I generally don't like lawyers, but you seem to be different. So I decided to help you. Take a look at these."

With that Dr. Ovita handed me a large brown envelope. It was about an inch thick. Out came six large color photographs showing Ernest's bloody fractured and splintered skull, then the sawing process to fit the plate and finally the stapling of the plate and then the closing of the wound with about fifty stitches. You could see a good portion of the exposed brain. It was gut wrenching. In fact, I had trouble controlling my stomach. I was breathing rapidly. Hold it—the judge might not let these pictures into evidence, since the defense would claim that they were unnecessary and designed to inflame the jury.

Dr. Ovita was no fool.

"I took these photos to protect myself should there be a malpractice claim. There often is, you know. They do accurately reflect what I found and what I did better than any verbal description I could give. I will require their use in order to testify. I think you can get them in as part of my operative record."

So, in the pretrial witness and exhibit list, I listed the photographs as exhibits under Dr. Ovita's name along with, and mixed in with, the "office records, x-rays, MRI's, photographs and narrative reports."

The trial date was approaching and Ernest was getting better and better. His family was glad to see him recover, but concerned that his case would evaporate. I met with Ernest. He was bright, charming, quite verbal, anxious to please and looked healthy and happy. He moved smoothly, listened, responded and almost had a twinkle in his eye. He probably was just glad to be alive.... "When can I go back to work?" The jury would not be inclined to be sympathetic.

"Ernest, you are not going to the trial. Your daughter, Cynthia, will sit in for you." (She was seventeen and cute as could be.)

"Mrs. Gomez, I don't want you at the trial either. Ernest looks too good. He is to stay at home. I'll try the case without him."

I must have been a little nuts, but with Cynthia sitting next to me at the table inside the railing in the courtroom I rose and spoke to the judge. The entire jury panel from which the jury would be selected was sitting in the back of the courtroom within earshot.

"Your Honor, I wish permission to have my client Ernest Gomez excused from attending his own trial, and permission to have his daughter, Cynthia, sit in his chair as his representative, so that I do not have a vacant seat next to me. Mrs. Gomez is at home with Mr. Gomez. In support of this request I would quote from the defense psychiatrist's sworn deposition as follows: 'Mr. Gomez should avoid the stress of trial. It would be very damaging to him. He should settle his case as soon as possible.' Your Honor, there have been no offers to settle this case."

The Court, Judge Patua, about sixty years old, an experienced judge, in black robe, leaning over the bench: "I will allow Cynthia to sit in for her father, Ernest Gomez."

We interviewed and impaneled the jury. We made opening statements. I told the jury that we were seeking punitive damages and that I intended to show that Millennium, based on their corporate statement, could well afford to pay punitive damages of ten million dollars. I explained that Mr. Gomez was psychiatrically not able to attend his own trial, and would never even be able to walk his daughter Cynthia down the aisle at her wedding. My voice "caught" in my throat. My eyes started to tear.

The State Trooper testified. The drunk driving "no contest" agreement went into evidence. The pictures of the crash were admitted and the first day of trial was ending.

The judge leans over the bench... He makes direct eye contact with me, drops his jaw...

"Mr. Ress. You mean that there were no offers of settlement?"

"None, Your Honor."

Judge Patua turns and stares at opposing counsel.

"Mr. McArthur. Is Mr. Ress accurate? No offers?"

McArthur shifts his weight, seems uncomfortable and says:

"Sir, I have no control over the client or the insurance carrier. In fact I represent the excess insurance company, Glacier. Global, the primary carrier, has denied coverage."

Judge Patua leans over the bench and stares at McArthur.

"McArthur, go back to your client and tell them that I want this case settled."

Day two started with various records custodians including Palmetto General Hospital.

I call the defense insurance company psychiatrist as an adverse witness and, limiting the area of questioning, ask him to confirm that Mr. Gomez was sufficiently fragile from an emotional point of view and that he should not be subjected to the stress of a trial. He agrees. The jury is on the edge of their seats.

Dr. Bianco leaves the courtroom and the judge calls us to the bench.

This time His Honor is leaning out over the high desk

"Mr. McArthur, do you have any authority."

"No, sir."

"Don't you understand?" (He points a finger.) "I said that I want this case settled and I want you to pay two point five million. Now."

"Your Honor, my client is only the excess carrier and they won't pay."

I join in.

"Your Honor, this is a ten-million-dollar case. We are seeking ten million and I can't accept two point five million."

The judge is now riled up. He stretches his jaw forward.

"You'll take it…. McArthur, tell your client to come up with it by tomorrow. I am not joking with you."

The judge gets up quickly and storms out of the courtroom.

I knew we had them. They couldn't flaunt the judge and not pay the price. He would allow me to introduce the assets of Millennium and allow a charge to the jury for punitive damages. McArthur will now have to report that huge ten-million-dollar damage exposure to Glacier as well as Global and Millennium. Then there were Dr. Ovita's pictures. Judge Patua would now probably allow them into evidence. It was a decision solely within his discretion. McArthur didn't even know that those pictures were coming at him.

"Judge, although this case is worth and we will seek ten million dollars, my client would accept three million plus taxable costs in an effort to cooperate with the Court."

God knows I would be thrilled to get one million. All the medical bills had already been paid by various insurance companies. Ernest was paid sick leave for his lost time from work. He was ready to go back to work and was remembering and speaking well. His eyesight had come back just fine, and he and his wife were planning on another child.

The judge was clearly irritated.

"Don't you gentlemen listen? I said two point five million and I want it tendered by tomorrow at nine a.m. Mr. McArthur, your client will pay it plus costs and seek reimbursement from Global. Mr. Ress, don't argue, just take it."

The bailiff calls the Court to order. It's nine thirty in the morning. We are all standing. The judge walks rapidly to his high-back leather chair. It's almost like a throne.

"OK Mr. McArthur do you have the money?"

"Yes sir, but only two million."

"You still don't understand me. I said two point five plus costs and I meant it. Now get on the phone now and get it. I mean now."

Five minutes late Mr. McArthur is back.

"Judge, I have it."

The judge leans forward. "Mr. Ress, OK?"

"Only if we have cleared funds within ten days."

The judge says to McArthur. "Don't argue, just do it… This case is settled."

Not so fast. Yes, I made a forty percent contingent fee, which equals one million dollars. I bought one million dollars of tax-free bonds yielding seven and a half percent annually. I bought them at seventy-two cents on the dollar and paid the income tax on the fees from other funds.

Glacier Insurance, the excess insurance company that had laid out the settlement money, sued Global, the basic insurance company, for bad faith for failing to tender the one million dollar basic policy which would have settled the case. McArthur called me as a witness. I looked at the jury, each one separately, as I told the story including our willingness initially to accept one million dollars and waiting at the phone on that Friday afternoon when no call came.

McArthur: "Mr. Ress, what made you think now that this case was worth over one million dollars?"

He knew that I had the settlement brochure at the ready. I brought it out and explained to the jury how it established that the case was worth three million dollars. But I didn't stop there.

I was looking directly at the jury and I said:

"Mr. McArthur, there is something else that I learned of later and was going to be introduced into evidence that really makes the value of this case much greater. These photographs taken by the treating brain surgeon, Dr. Ovita."

Before Global's attorney could object, I took out the photos and held them up and showed them to the jury. They gasped. You could clearly hear the unified gasp. Global's attorney stood there dumbfounded and the pictures went into evidence.

The verdict against my pals at Global was for five million five hundred thousand dollars.

Glacier's attorney called about a month later and offered to pay ten thousand dollars to me for my expert testimony, or to donate to my favorite charity.

"No thank you." I already had my reward.

It's not over.

Mrs. Gomez makes an appointment. She comes into the office with Mr. Gomez. She is clearly nervous. She twists the ends of her purse strap and her fingers continue to move over one another as she speaks.

"Mr. Ress, Ernest is anxious to have a full life. We are expecting another child. He doesn't wish to use the cane anymore. He wants to drive the car. He wants to engage in sports and to go back to full-time work, which would involve strenuous activity. My friends warn that Global could have Ernest followed and try to set aside the settlement because he is so active and doing the things he said he could not do in his sworn statement."

I lean forward and smiled at them.

"Mrs. Gomez, normally I would not say this, but Millennium and Global have done us both a wrong. They should have been apologetic and reasonable. The Millennium people are nasty, selfish, prejudiced drunkards. Global let me wait for a phone call that never came. They are mean people. You are devout Catholics. Have you ever heard of Sainte-Anne-de-Beaupré? It's a church near Quebec. It's famous for its miraculous cures. You might consider a trip there. The walls are lined with crutches. It would be a good place to pray for a cure with a priest and leave the cane."

20

Mediation

This is a story about two mediations that I conducted. The first was with Israelis and the second with Greeks, but before you hear about what happened you should know a little about the mediation process and its shortcomings. I'll try to make it brief and to the point.

Did you know that you don't have to be a lawyer to be a United States Supreme Court Associate Justice or even Chief Justice? Nor do you have to be an attorney in order to be a mediator, even though it involves legal knowledge and ability to reason as a lawyer and is part of the judicial system. All you have to do is take a course which can be completed in two weekends, pay the State licensing fee and there it is! You're a Florida State Certified Mediator. You can put the title on your stationery, have a professional business card printed and put letters after your signature. Mediation, a simple process to resolve disputes, which was initially conducted as sort of an informal proceeding by the village elders or the monarch or sheik, has become a self-made labyrinth with its own complex language which often is used to confuse the simplest of things and from which people create a lifetime occupation.

Mediators are often uneducated and inadequately trained and by their numbers they become the owners of the mediation "process." These "Certified" mediators have their own clubs or associations just like the lawyers' Bar associations. They are regulated by the State with dues, licensing and continuing education requirements and have meetings and conventions. They have their own journals and write technical, erudite articles about how disputes are settled. In fact some of the law schools have actually created professorships of "dispute resolution."

However, you can be a self-proclaimed mediator and you don't even need to be certified or have any training at all. There may be no applicable control over what you do, no license nor educational requirement and no disciplinary controls. It's like practicing law or psychology without a license, but it's lawful. Evidently, mediation is not a real, fully recognized profession.

One of the problems is the corruption of the "process" by mediators who are not objective, but who look out for their own personal interests and beliefs at the expense of the parties. One of these is the family law mediator who has religious beliefs or gender bias that override his or her objectivity in dissolution of marriages cases.

Another is the mediator who thrives on repeat business and in reality silently works for the repeat customer, often an insurance company. Take, for example, the retired judge who meets with the insurance mediation "specialist" and is told the "number" that the insurance company wants to pay in order to close the file. In this instance, say, eight thousand dollars. Then the judge, tall, thin, white-haired, with a white moustache, dressed in a dark suit with a white shirt and a bow tie, meets with the young injured plaintiff who is wearing a T-shirt and his inexperienced, informally dressed young attorney and tells them how weak their case is. The mediator stands over them while they are seated and speaks of his impressive career on the bench and tells them how many cases just like this he has presided over and how little this case is worth. Why, based on his vast experience, they have a good chance of losing entirely. He says that they should consider taking one thousand dollars and "run." He gets them to agree to accept four thousand dollars. He then excuses himself and talks to the insurance company representative privately.

"I've got them down to six thousand and will keep working. You can close your file. This one is under control."

Back to the plaintiff's attorney:

"The insurance company is willing to go to three thousand and that's it."

The young injured man says to take it and the case is settled.

Back to the insurance company lady.

"You can thank me. I really worked at it and got them to take three thousand. We should both look good."

The judge gets to mediate at least three cases every week for this insurance company and never discloses this ongoing relationship.

The corporate mediator has a primary interest in protecting his or her employer and keeping his job. They do as they are told by their employer. They have no hesitation in misquoting the prevailing law. Sometimes one of the parties pays for the cost of the mediation, including the mediator's fee. Who do you think the mediator is going to appreciate more? Would you ever dream of having one side pay a judge's salary? And a judge, or even an arbitrator, would rarely, almost never, ask any of the parties on both sides to confide in him and to trust him and to disclose the most confidential information. Judges just don't do that. Yet mediators regularly say:

" You have to trust me. Tell me the lowest number that you would accept and I'll try to get it for you."

Every smart attorney knows that "manipulating the mediator" is the game to be played. They never fully trust the mediator and never disclose the true amounts they would pay or accept. They often flatter, threaten, lie or even get up and walk toward the door in order to impress the mediator. Defense lawyers and commercial litigators are getting paid by the hour, and are in general not anxious to resolve litigation. They make their money by enlarging disputes, getting their clients worked up and in a fighting mode. By closing their files they end the cash flow from that case.

There also is a belief that the case can almost always be resolved at a subsequent mediation, creating additional attorneys' fees, so just let this one go by unless there is a time constraint or great economic need or the lawyer needs the settlement fee in order to make an alimony payment. The mediator pulls out his "bag of tricks." He enthusiastically agrees with each of the parties in private. He reassures them of the integrity of their position and of their high character. He uses the word "we" instead of the word "you." However, sometimes, in private, he tears their case apart. Sometimes he tries browbeating them. Whatever works. He plays the game.

Sometimes I would ask the aggressive defense attorney, who was trying his best to kill the settlement, to estimate the future number of hours he or she would need to conclude the case. They couldn't go too low because the client was listening and would remember when the final bill was presented.

"So you think you can get this resolved in fifty more hours? There will be depositions, pretrial Motions with court hearings, meetings with witnesses... You are looking at a two-day trial, with your client taking time away from the business. I think that you should leave yourself much more leeway. You are certainly worth three hundred an hour and taking your extremely conservative estimate, that would mean that it would cost the client no less than fifteen thousand dollars to win, but there is a chance of losing. The other side is willing to accept thirteen thousand to settle this case right now. This appears to be a 'no brainer'."

When the people are out of the room and the lawyer has left, the client thanks me.

The Israelis

Some of the lawyers I had worked with knew that as a mediator I might be able to get their less desirable cases settled. A friend who was a Judge of the County Court, with jurisdiction up to fifteen thousand dollars, was planning to retire. He sent me all of his cases, hopefully to be resolved. I became as busy as I wanted to be. Most of the mediations were simple collection matters where the multiple excuses for nonpayment varied widely from claims of "defective goods" to late delivery, but the real issue was generally the inability to pay and the questionable "collectability" of the defendant. The standard settlement formula was to provide for a compromise sum, making periodic payments with a provision that the full original claimed amount plus interest and attorneys' fees would come due and a judgment would be entered if there was a default. I cleared the judge's calendar. He said that he tried only two cases in two years.

This case was quite different. The mediation was scheduled in my small unpretentious office with a long white marble conference table, which actually was my former desk. It was a big comedown for me. No teakwood paneling. No thick carpets. Although it was new, "drab" was the word for it. One secretary-receptionist. I had read the summaries the three sets of attorneys had earlier sent in. The divorced couple owned a three-story office building with a restaurant on the ground floor. Neither wanted to sell their share and the restaurant owner wanted more space and a new lease. They were all fighting wildly, the owners with one another, and both with the restaurant owner.

The middle-aged Israeli couple sat in my waiting area, in which my secretary's gray metal desk and some file cabinets occupied the bulk of the small space, and which hardly had room for them, just two chairs. Their attorneys were standing. They all were glaring at one another. (*Get them separated as soon as possible*—one of my self-made rules—went through my head.) I put the husband and his lawyer into my small side office and sat the wife and her attorney in my conference room. The husband was somewhat overweight, with curly dark hair showing some gray. The former wife was conservatively dressed in a tan business suit. Her black hair was pulled back tight and she was wearing metal-rimmed glasses. I could picture her firing an Uzi while throwing hand grenades in the Israeli army. (*Stay objective. Don't tilt.*) Next there appeared the glamour girl restaurant owner, also an Israeli, dressed in a satin skirt and blouse combination with three-inch heels, more suited for a dinner club than my modest mediation rooms. Joan's blond hair was piled high and the mascara was heavy. Her attorney was wearing a vest. (*Don't make quick unfair judgments.*) I thought... Keep them in the waiting area.

The husband, Victor, was a doctor, a cardiologist. (*He should take better care of himself. He's just on the edge of fat. There you go, forming opinions without a foundation.*) The ex-wife was a realtor and I would not have wanted to bargain with her. The restaurant owner, the overdressed blonde, (*oops*) was the doctor's former girlfriend, while he was married. They all were Israeli. (*I didn't like any of them. Why should I knock myself out trying to untie this bird's nest of a knot?*)

Have all parties and their attorneys present when the lawyers make opening statements. (*Try to have them agree to be civil to one another, to listen to the other side and to work with me in order to get the case settled.*) I talk to them:

"Sometimes a less than perfect settlement is worth more than a protracted and expensive fight."

I talk to them some more—about the "confidentiality" of the mediation and that they can't tell anyone about what went on here, including the judge, and that after the opening statements they are free to leave any time they want.

"Is it alright to call one another by first names?"

I try to get them talking to me, but they grumbled and answered in grunts and monosyllables. I could tell that the hatred was boiling. These were very angry people.

After the attorneys make the opening statements, it's usually best to get the parties away from each other into separate rooms where I can talk to them alone. This is called a "caucus", another pseudo term for a private meeting. This is the time for "venting." (That's my word.) It means, like a psychiatrist, you have the party you are meeting with verbalize all their poison, vitriol, hatred, resentment and frustration, and you listen attentively. Making lots of notes looks good even though you don't need them. My experience is that until they each vigorously complain out loud, you'll never get the case settled. By the way, it's always smart to sit as near the door as you can so that when a frustrated party opens fire or pulls a knife you can get out of there fast. That's not in the "Mediator's Manual."

My first meeting was with Zelda, the wife and her attorney. If she could have killed both of them with one shot she would probably have done so. She had no trouble venting.

"I hate that bastard. While I was cooking for him he was screwing that bitch. I'll never agree to anything that he wants."

The meeting with the doctor and his lawyer wasn't much better.

"She is a nasty, calculating, mean person who cannot be trusted. Whatever she proposes will be tilted for her and against me. I hope she drops."

At first I thought that he was talking about his ex-wife, Zelda, then I wasn't so sure.

Joan, the tenant, was angry.

"He said he would marry me. Now he won't even get my lease renewed. I need more space. The fixtures are built in and can't be removed. I have a fortune in the kitchen alone. I hate both of them."

I don't like to meet too long privately with any of the parties because the others get worked up and resent waiting for their turn. (*Limit your time to five or ten minutes, then get back to the other party*.) My job was getting clearer. If I could get the husband and wife to settle their real-estate dispute then maybe I could get a lease for the former girlfriend and then maybe they'll all go down to the sea and live happily ever after. Fat chance!

The attorney with the vest, Joan's lawyer, had the plans for the building. I asked him:

"What would your client like to see happen with regard to the restaurant?"

Of course he came up with a plan and proposal. His client needed a fifty percent increase in space and wanted a new lease with low rental and a long term with options to renew. (I would like that too.)

"What about using the roof upstairs?"

"We're interested."

Even if Joan's plan was good, it couldn't appear to come from her. Zelda and Victor would make short work of it. They would rather have half the building vacant than to concede anything to Joan. If it was proposed too soon it would never fly. It could only be considered after extensive argument and making the landlords believe that it was actually their idea. Also, Joan had to think that she outsmarted Victor. Any resolution providing for a buy-sell or division of the building between Zelda and Victor was like the Palestinians receiving an Israeli peace proposal with open arms. Forget it!

I went back and forth with the set of plans trying to sense what I could settle. (*Try to get them to agree on something, anything, in order to get the ball rolling.*) We had been at it for hours and hours, all day. The solution was becoming clearer by virtue of elimination. Neither Zelda nor Victor would ever sell to one another and neither wanted to sell to a third person. So we're talking partition (dividing the building physically).

The time for the mediation ran out. Surprisingly, they all agreed to reschedule and they showed up a week later, a little less angry, but still spitting bullets. I gave credit for the proposed partition solution to the parties and their attorneys, but privately.

"Victor, your idea of possibly splitting the building was really wise and although I still don't think the other side would ever agree to it, it's worth a try."

Then to Zelda's attorney:

"You know the thought you had of possibly dividing the building physically and working out a lease was going nowhere, but I think it's worth trying again."

They didn't really oppose the restaurant lease, although Victor was afraid of Joan. He didn't want her calling him with the pretense being the status of the lease or the condition of the property. He was glad that Zelda would deal with Joan. The women even seemed to be getting along. After all, they had many things in common, among them their intimacy with Victor.

Zelda agreed that the building could be divided into two sections with very little renovation. The air conditioning and heating would basically remain the same. The elevators would be shared, as well as the common areas and parking. Zelda could take the side that contained the restaurant. There was a dumbwaiter going to the roof as well as an elevator, and there was a small structure with plumbing already located on the roof, three floors above the restaurant.

The idea was an outdoor rooftop garden café—which could ultimately be enclosed—serving cocktails, with dinner brought up on the dumbwaiter. Much more space would be available with little or no expense to the owners. The renovation costs could be financed and the increased rent would cover the payments plus a profit. Joan would sign and personally guaranty the lease.

A "common area" monthly payment would make up for any increase in taxes or insurance. The facility would be used primarily at night with little interference or inconvenience to the other tenants, and it would be a place to have a drink before heading home. The new extended lease would provide for a portion of the rent going to Victor for parking fees and signage and to balance the income.

I can't tell you how many hours of marking up the plans and negotiating the lease and outlining documents, including time schedules, it took. A lot. But once they got into it everyone became enthusiastic to get the challenging problems solved and the hatred started to wane. They began to talk to one another in a civil tone and they each became more reasonable and cooperative and fair. It became a psychodrama, like acting out roles in a Broadway play. It was almost unbelievable.

It all came to pass. An extensive contract was drawn and executed. The property was divided, with an agreement by Victor and Zelda to leave the building to their child when they died. The lease was signed. I never thought that it would happen. I had never seen such bare hatred and animosity. It's hard to believe, even today. They shook hands at the end. I thought that they had paid a dear price for making peace. They had been deprived of their major joy and their all-consuming passion in life, which had been to despise one another.

Well, if THEY can do it, the mediation "Process" is available and there's hope for the Israelis and Palestinians.

The Greeks

It was another one of those impossible mediations. Marko Thoros was seventy-nine years old and dead. He died slowly of cancer and his final days were spent at a hospice facility. His son Alex, age fifty, an independently wealthy man, came in from Chicago and was here in Miami for over a month with his dad until he passed. The stepmother and second wife, Anna, had nursed Marko and was attentive to him until he went to hospice. She told Marko that she didn't want him to return to the house. She was alone at home when Marko died. Marko wanted to die at home, but Anna said: "No. I don't want him in the house when he dies." Alex never forgave her. Thus started the battle of the child from the first marriage and the stepmother.

It had been a long second marriage, twenty years. Marko and Anna met through mutual friends when he was in Greece about a year after his first wife died of a heart attack. Anna was forty years old and lived in Athens and agreed to come to Miami. The new marriage went quite well. They were more than compatible. They actually adored and respected one another. It was too late for children, but they traveled to Greece every year and built a beautiful two-story Mediterranean style house in Coral Gables on an oversized lot with six mature cypress trees in the front, and a large patio and a kidney-shaped pool in the back.

They dined out often, mostly at Greek restaurants where they were greeted as "family." In other words, they had a full and happy life together with no real problems. Marko was a wealthy and influential man.

Alex wasn't pleased about the fact that his father remarried less than two years after his mother died. He was even less happy with the terms of his father's will, which left Anna the large house and three-quarters of everything else. After all, he was the only blood-related heir and she had moved into the family, and when Anna didn't come to the hospice and refused to allow Marko to die at home, Alex was livid and able to turn Marko against Anna. Alex's lawyers, a high-priced firm, flew down from Chicago and went to the hospice. With their guidance Marko signed a new will leaving the bulk of his estate to Alex and giving Anna the minimum allowed by law. Anna was suing to set aside this most recent will.

The law in Florida was in issue as to whether there is a presumption of undue influence when the beneficiary's own attorney prepares the will in the beneficiary's favor. The person proposing the enforcement of the will would have the burden to prove that it was not obtained by undue influence and to establish circumstances that would explain the will's provisions. This was going to be quite a fight. The son, Alex, came to the mediation with three sets of attorneys. Anna came in with a high-priced local firm.

They were ready to go at one another. Anna also brought her brother to the mediation. He was a Bishop of the Greek Orthodox Church in full regalia—a big black cylindrical hat, a full black cassock with a wide silk sash and a large crucifix on his chest.

Formidable! No one objected to him being in the room.

The battle commenced. Anna finally explained that she herself had been diagnosed with cancer and her breasts had just been removed and she had thought that she was dying, and didn't want Marko to learn of it before he died. That was why she didn't want him at home. The discussions became heated. In private meetings they each accused the other of being selfish and caring only for Marko's money. The lawyers each had briefs on the law, which seemed to me to be in great issue. Anna's lawyers wanted to set aside the last will and go back to the document, which favored Anna. Alex's lawyers stood behind the legality and effectiveness of the latest hospice will.

After about five hours I had everyone seated in my conference room, including the Bishop. I turned to all of them.

"Who here is representing Marko Thoros?

There was sudden silence.

"What are you talking about? My dad is dead."

That was Alex.

"Yes, what are you getting at? Mr. Thoros is gone."

That was the Bishop.

"*I* am representing Marko Thoros."

That was ME.

"*I* speak for Marko Thoros... and Marko Thoros says: 'I see my loving son fighting with my loving wife and I am very upset'."

I addressed them all:

"All of you: listen! Marko Thoros' soul is in limbo. He cannot attain heaven because his family, who he loves so much, is fighting and he cannot find peace. He cannot enter into a 'state of grace' and ascend to heaven."

The Bishop rose to his feet and proclaimed loudly:

"He's absolutely right. Shame on us."

The son, Alex and the wife Anna both looked at me and Alex said:

"I'll do anything you say, Mr. Ress. You decide."

Anna said:

"I agree. We are wrong to do this. You decide. Yes, you decide."

"I'm not allowed to make a decision for you, but I know that Marko would want you to just divide everything equally, but more importantly, to embrace one another and kiss one another and look after one another in honor of Marko Thoros."

They had their arms around one another when they kissed and agreed.

21

Divorces

Shades of Gray

The Grays, Tom and Anita, were splitting. They had lots of money, no kids and the dog had died. It should have been a relatively simple case, just divide their marital assets and work out an alimony agreement. No. Not that easy. Angry divorcing couples need to vent their frustrations. They always seem to find an issue to wrangle over. Each wants to get the better of the other. Often it finds its way into to the details of child custody. Who can pick up the child? Where can the wife live? Is it to be joint custody or just visitation? Sometimes they fight bitterly over who gets the dog or the cat. The wealthier they are the meaner some of these issues become, and an enormous number of lawyer's hours are spent on these vendettas.

Mrs. Gray was independently well off, being an heiress of the Fontana fortune. Fontana beauty products. She was fairly flexible in negotiating the financial arrangements because she really didn't care that much and we were only about three hundred thousand dollars apart from a settlement, but she did want the oil painting of "Randy" their deceased Boston Terrier. Tom said "No way! That's MY painting." Tom was the CEO and owner of Gray Tool Co., now located in Cleveland, Ohio, which started out with two employees. He and Anita would wind up with six hundred workers. Around and around they went. They wouldn't even agree to my suggestion of having the painting copied by a famous artist and picking lots as to who kept the original. I was getting annoyed with them, particularly Tom, who was acting as a selfish, spoiled child and arrogant boss all in one.

Vincento Vascelli, the senior partner of Vascelli, Eagleton and Sofer called me.

"Ress, I represent Gray Tool Company here in Cleveland and I have been asked to take over representing Tom Gray in this divorce case. I suggest that you and Mrs. Gray come up here right now and meet with me and Mr. Gray in an effort to get this matter resolved."

"Mr. Vascelli, I'm in the middle of a trial and would appreciate your scheduling the meeting in about two weeks."

"Mr. Ress, I think you should come up right now. What about this Saturday? It should be over in one day. You'll be home Saturday night. I promise."

My client wanted it over and now. So, OK. It would be in three days, on Saturday.

Anita and I flew up late Friday night. She was quite an attractive woman, although I now remember that she walked with a decided limp. She wore simple, but expensively tailored suits with real silk blouses, a small gold and diamond brooch and had low-cut shoes with short heels. She was a brunette, five feet three inches tall, trim, about thirty-five years old and very pretty. We checked into the Raleigh Hotel, the nice old, elegant downtown social center, and I made it a point to have her room on the tenth floor and mine on the second. Tom was not above using surveillance to embarrass his wife. We discussed our strategy. Our financial analysis included an adjustment for Anita having helped found the tool business. She wanted it over. The next morning at nine we were in Mr. Vascelli's office. The conference room was huge, twenty-foot high ceilings, heavy everything—drapes with gold tassels, oak furniture, tapestries on the walls and yes, believe it or not, a Degas ballet dancer statue. This three-foot-high cast bronze with tutu was the real thing.

In walks Mr. Vascelli, making his appearance, and he looked just like the "Don" from Sicily: about sixty years old, white hair, six feet three inches, two hundred and fifty pounds, with vest, cravat, pocket watch and heavy cufflinks. Tom sits next to him. Anita and I sit across the big table. Mr. Vascelli wanted to talk money and was willing to up the ante one hundred thousand dollars. Mr. Gray wanted to talk about the painting and insisted that it be his and his alone. I told them that we would keep the painting and wouldn't take less than the three hundred thousand dollars already demanded. By three in the afternoon, my suggestion of having the painting copied and then exchanging the original and the copy every six months was accepted.

Mr. Vascelli announced that Tom wanted to have dinner with his wife tonight and that if Tom's date was satisfactory they would consider increasing their offer. Mr. Vascelli said that we should meet on Sunday, after church, at ten in the morning. I was not happy, but Anita, who spoke in that soft slow voice that is cultivated in the best families and at the finest schools, said that she preferred that the negotiations be completed.

I knew with whom I was dealing and the power plays to expect, but I had a plan of my own. They could have closed today, resolved the money issue by paying two hundred thousand and saved one hundred thousand dollars, but they wanted to play me like a hooked fish. No way!

"Anita, I have a surprise for Mr. Vascelli and your husband, and if it's alright with you I will just do it and you should be happy. We've already computed the value of your having worked at Gray Tool."... and I went on to explain what I intended to do.

"Mr. Ress, do whatever you wish, but I would like it resolved."

At ten after ten, Mr. Vascelli and Mr. Gray appeared.

"Mr. Ress, my client had a nice visit with his wife last night and we are prepared to offer to settle for two hundred thousand dollars."

"Mr. Vascelli, the price is now four hundred thousand dollars. My Saturday nights are very meaningful to me."

Tom Gray had to be physically restrained by his attorney, who said:

"Tom, do not underestimate Mr. Ress, he obviously has some basis for this new demand."

"Thank you, Mr. Vascelli. Please take a look at these pleadings. We are very much aware that there is a merger being consummated which was not disclosed to us, and that Gray Tool is being acquired by Boise Cascade. This is a lawsuit which will be filed tomorrow wherein Mrs. Gray will seek fifty percent of the stock of Gray Tool, since she was a founder and worked for Gray Tool Company and was never compensated. You can see that the lawsuit is here in Cuyahoga County and seeks to halt the

Boise Cascade merger and determine the ownership interest of Mrs. Gray."

Vascelli marched his client out of the room with his hand under Mr. Gray's arm. It didn't take ten minutes for Mr. Vascelli to convince his client. I was on a plane late that afternoon with a smiling Mrs. Gray.

My fee of three hundred thousand dollars was used towards buying our own office building. Anita, against my advice, invested her divorce money in a theatrical production which lasted one night at the Dade County Auditorium.

She still trades paintings of "Randy" every six months.

Don't Blame Me

Chuck and Arnold were double brothers-in-law. Chuck was married to Arnold's sister, Alice. Arnold was married to Chuck's sister, Lois. They, all four, all got along quite well and the boys went into business together, Fantasy Beauty Supplies. Fantasy had three delivery trucks and a retail store with storage in the back. Chuck and Arnold each made customer deliveries to a number of beauty salons and came into contact with many glamour girls.

It didn't take long for both of them to start having sex with their customers, sometimes in the back room of the store.

One night Alice noticed that Chuck had lipstick on his work shirt collar. She decided to follow him. The next day she walked in on him just as a young blonde was putting on her dress and leaving the back room of the beauty supply store.

That night she summoned a family meeting and she, Chuck,

Lois and Arnold sat down.

"I asked you all here because I caught Chuck screwing a blonde and it's over. Our marriage is over. Since we are in business together it's going to affect all of us. The business is going to be dissolved. Chuck, you bastard. You caused all of this!"

Chuck pointed his finger at Arnold.

"Why are you picking on me? Why are you blaming me? Arnold started all of it by screwing the redhead and half of the other customers."

The girls wanted to know if I could combine the cases and save them some costs and fees.

From Russia With Love

Charlie Osgood was a ski club buddy of mine. He actually lived in Philadelphia, but he kept an apartment and a seventy-foot yacht in Miami. Charlie became involved in helping a Russian family immigrate into the United States. He was able to get the parents and then their children into America. The younger child was a beautiful twenty-year-old blue-eyed blonde with a knockout figure and a dazzling smile. Charlie, who was about fifty-two years old, flipped out over her. She had learned English and was deeply indebted to Charlie as were her parents and brother. She married him.

Charlie owned real estate in Philadelphia including an apartment complex. He also owned an ostrich farm. He entertained on his yacht and Olga, who was studying at the University of Miami, would dance on the front deck with some of her girlfriends. The music would be loud and wild. Olga was finishing her last year at the "U" and my wife and I didn't think that Charlie was in a stable marriage; however, he was happy and she seemed satisfied with the relationship.

It was about two weeks before Olga's graduation when Charlie called me in the office.

"Lewis, this is a personal call for advice, so don't bill me. I need your advice as a friend. Olga wants out... and she wants one hundred thousand dollars. That goddamn rotten little whore. I don't want to give her one goddamn cent. I want to fight her all the way. What do I do?"

"Charlie, how long were you married? Three years.... and how often did you have sex with Olga... three times a week. She's worth at least three hundred dollars a pop. That's the least a judge will award her. Then there are the attorneys' fees. She's got nothing, so you'll pay her lawyers and it will be at least one hundred thousand before they are done with you. Then there are your attorney's fees of at least fifty thousand bucks. You're up to one hundred and fifty thousand and you haven't given her a dime. She'll get something. So just add what you think is reasonable on top. Also you will have made an enemy of her. She'll hate you.

If I were you I'd call her in and tell her that you love her and will give her the one hundred thousand and then give her a ten thousand dollars tip. I'm serious."

I didn't hear from Charlie for about six months. When he did call me he was extremely grateful.

"Lewis, you saved me! I called Olga in and told her that I was going to pay her the one hundred thousand and in addition I was giving her a ten thousand dollar tip. She started to cry with happiness and gratitude. She visits me once a week at least and gives me blow jobs and wild sex and I don't have to support her."

22

What is a Satyr?

Most people don't know what a satyr is. Maybe you've seen pictures of the man, not half-animal, but a man with ram's horns and a tail and a huge penis. It is very male. He is lecherous. In other words it's a guy who can't get enough. Enough sex. Is it just a Greek myth or is it for real?

Allow me to assure you that it is real. Some say that it is an illness and that it might make a good psychiatric defense in a criminal court. The disease is called "satyriasis." So I guess my friends Don and Larry were sick long before that illness affected the behavior of a bunch of our male corporate executives, United States Senators, Congressmen and many past and even the present President. None of them was smart enough to call it a medical disease and to get off the hook with the promise of seeking treatment.

Don was a doctor, a well-known, highly respected medical specialist. He propositioned women that he met on airplanes, nurses, patients, young, old, short, fat, white, black and everything in between. In the days that I am talking about they had just invented "the pill." There was very little sexual disease going around and there was a wild scramble by women to feel free.

148

They would become the aggressors, calling guys on the phone asking for dates. Women were burning their bras. There were no exams or x-ray machines at the airports. Some women went on airplanes and weren't wearing underpants. The chiropractor on the ground floor of our office building was sexually "adjusting" many of his patients, including his best friend's wife. Marijuana was all over the place. It was like a huge carnal celebration. Like the end of Prohibition. Don also had access to hard drugs and he supplied wealthy, celebrity patients with "pain medication." You would easily recognize their names. One of them, a famous vocalist, tried to sing at Don's funeral, but was too hoarse. She was rasping and croaking. She died of an overdose not too long after the funeral. That is the setting for the story about my friend Larry, the satyr.

Larry was young, thin but wiry, about my age, thirty at the time, with blondish hair, light skin and a small but slightly bulbous nose. His blue eyes were dancing most of the time. He spoke softly and had a lilt to his voice. His clothes fit like a glove. He usually wore English shirts with French cuffs and pleated slacks. His alligator loafers had real gold Gucci emblems—and no socks, if you please. Of course he had a diamond Rolex and a star sapphire pinky ring. He had a customized gold money clip. Women thought that he looked like Elvis and he had a cute smile, too.

Larry hadn't always been like that. He came out of the trailer parks. He started off leaving school early and working in construction, with a hammer and a saw. He learned how to operate machinery; first, trucks of all kinds and then bulldozers, and ultimately draglines. Those are big excavating machines with heavy tank treads, with a long trestle steel arm and cables running from the cab where the driver sits, up the arm and then through a roller, down to a large metal bucket. They were designed to pick up piles of material, often sand, in the bucket and deposit it either into a dump truck or on another pile of material. Larry scraped up enough money to buy a used dump truck and started hauling fill when he was eighteen. He had two trucks and then three and then a second hand D-3 bulldozer and finally a small used dragline. He was twenty-one when he bid on his first government job. It was a disaster. Besides mechanical breakdowns, he had underestimated the extent and difficulty of the dirt removal and it became clear that he was going to go into default. He was facing bankruptcy and had personally guaranteed the job instead of getting a performance bond.

He visited the government contracting office and begged for some relief. The project superintendent was a very solidly built, handsome, middle-aged woman who was sexually attracted to him. She devoured him with her eyes. He was cute. He was very sexy and Larry could have taught at the "method" school of acting. He was contrite and sweet and schoolboy charming. As she went around the desk she brushed against him. She put her hand on his shoulder and when she felt no resistance on his lower back, then his buttocks. She had a small black leather couch in her office and her own bathroom. It was a very hot affair in every way. They had intercourse twice a day—in her office on the couch, on the floor and on the desk, in his pickup truck, in the cab of the dragline and everyplace that you could imagine except her bed, since they never knew when her husband would be home. The supervisor conducted Larry through a little-known process to assist and protect first-time government contractors. With the guidance of the supervisor his contract was amended and adjusted to award additional funds and lengthen the time for performance. She also arranged for a large cash advance to be authorized. Larry was saved.

Larry started bidding on Florida State Highway construction through the Department of Transportation. That's when he met and partnered with Ricky Elmont. The company was known as Elmont and Basket or "E&B, Inc." Ricky had been around for a while and knew how to arrange to be the low bidder. He explained to Larry how Manny Levin got to control all the road jobs in Palm Beach County. Levin Construction was "king" in Palm Beach. Secret payment, subcontracts or other compensation was given to the other bidders so that they would bid high. You slipped in just under them. Then there was the appeal process to amend the contract as it went along in order to get the big profits. The subsoil was found to be different than the specifications in the bid. The amounts of muck (mud) were significantly greater than as represented in the contract. You had photos and tests and surveys from friendly sources to prove it. Manny Levin lived in a palace on the Ocean in Palm Beach and mingled with the socialites, so why not us?

After my law partner George Case became President of Great Bahama Island Enterprises he introduced me to Larry, who was dredging the Harbor in Freeport. Larry retained me and I had been representing him for a few months. Initially he didn't talk a lot about women or sex, but he had a sixteen-year-old girlfriend living in his apartment in the Bahamas and he disappeared for hours at a stretch, No one could reach him. No one knew where he was. There were no cell phones or pagers then. One day we were sitting in his very large office in Fort Lauderdale. Larry's feet were up on his antique desk, which had gold eagles on the top corners, when he grinned and said: "It's been two hours and I haven't been laid." He used his forefinger and thumb to pull his French cuffs out of his jacket sleeves and I noticed two beautifully worked gold cufflinks with small diamonds. He thumbed through a small phone directory with his manicured fingers, dialed and picked up the phone. The conversation was quite unexpectedly short:

"Hi darlin'. You guessed it. I'd love to…. Yes, right now. I'll be there soon. Miss you. Bye."

Larry looked at me with a boyish grin.

"She's got the sweetest pussy…" And he went on with a detailed description of the lady's pubic hair, its color, its softness. "Like silk." Then he gave me a full description of her body, from head to toe.

Before he excused himself he'd arranged for a late afternoon meeting with a married woman and a dinner date with a secretary from a doctor's office. He insisted on telling me about each woman's sexual preferences, their favorite positions and of course the color of their pubic hair and whether it was curly. He discussed the "bikini" haircut and how some women dyed their pubic hair to achieve a match with their other tresses.

He was still going at it over two times a day.

Ricky Elmont was, before Larry bought him out, an expert on business entertainment. The party always had the same elements and the guests never seem to tire of it. There had to be booze. Plenty of booze. And there had to be "broads," plenty of broads. Besides Larry's personal stable, he had lists of professionals, semi-professionals, party girls and nice girls looking to get married. And there should be food and some type of entertainment. A live band was always good. No records. No photographs, and the guys should be people with whom Larry was doing or wanted to do business. The best places were hotels.

The first party to which I was invited, and felt compelled to attend, was at the Miami Springs Villas. Larry had a relationship with Carole, a very nice redhead. She was an older woman, probably around forty, who arranged for eight professionals to entertain the guests. The party started off in a small private room with a guitar player. There was a buffet table, but nothing special. Then it happened. The older woman called for everyone's attention. Then she introduced her girlfriends one at a time, telling a little bit about her including the fact that she went to college. Each was young, trim, attractive, and would be assigned to one of the eight guests.

"Please tell the gentlemen your name and where you went to college."

Most of the eight guys hadn't finished high school. I don't think they ever read a book or even a newspaper other than the sports section. They were impressed.

"I'm Anita and I went to Florida State."

"Sandra.... and I'm a 'Nole too."

"I'm Carla and I went to Vassar College."

"My name is Shirley and I went to Smith, but only for two years."

Most of the rest said that they were Florida State graduates. Frankly, I didn't believe any of it, especially that a Vassar graduate would become a hooker.

After a few drinks they went off with their dates into separate rooms in the villa. I was left with a lady who clearly was as unhappy with me as I was with her. It was instant mutual dislike. She looked me up and down. I am about five feet six inches tall. The other guys were six footers. She said:

"You're strictly J.V."

That means worse than second string. I was stunned by the insult from a prostitute. I started to feel warm all over. My face turned red. I was offended. I was hurt, but I kept my mouth shut. Then a feeling of relief came over me and I smiled.

"You're right. I am strictly J.V. Let's just have a drink."

She immediately picked up on it and seemed relieved. We talked a little and the next thing that happened was that the group came back into the room and there was what could only be called an orgy. There were at least four couples changing partners and fornicating on various couches or on the floor. Larry was making it with the older woman. I slipped out since I knew half of the men and didn't want to be known by any of the women. What I found out later was interesting. Carole was the personnel director at an exclusive employment agency. They advertised in Coral Gables and South Miami for housewives who wanted to make substantial compensation as "social hostesses," working afternoons only. The agency was highly discreet and in fact Carole was the owner. I never saw any of them again.

There was no getting out of Larry's Christmas party. It was at Pier 66. This time I had a good idea of what was coming, but Larry was paying me the equivalent of one thousand dollars an hour way back then, and he was not a man to be turned down. Surprisingly enough it was quite straight. There was a five-piece band. Larry's secretary, Dolores, escorted me into a ballroom with about sixty people including some very conservatively dressed young women and introduced me to some of Larry's business associates, including Jake Raven. He was friendly, wearing a dark-gray business suit, clearly custom fitted, and included me in the conversation he was having with three very lovely women. Jake had just finished a one-year jail term for bid rigging He had taken the rap for his boss, Manny Levin. I noticed that there were no waiters and the drinks were "help yourself" with no bartenders. Also there were some very big men standing at the door.

After about thirty minutes the doors were closed. Nobody else seemed to notice.. They were busy drinking and talking. The band was playing. Two extremely beautiful girls started to embrace at the side of the room. At first they seemed to be dancing. They kissed one another on the lips. Their hands roamed over one another including fondling one another's breasts and rubbing one another on the behind. They undressed one another and somehow as if it was contagious, other women in the party started taking off their clothes. It didn't take that long for all of the thirty women to disrobe. The men were naked too. The two original ladies started to kiss one another in the crotch. A hand grabbed my shoulder. Then it engaged my arm.

"We're out of here!"

It was Larry's secretary, Dolores. She hustled me into the foyer and said that my wife had already been told to expect me home within an hour.

"What is going on in there?... How did that happen?...Who are these people?"

Dolores told me. Some of the men were mid-level executives of the Department of Transportation and the women were a mix and mingle of six prostitutes, six party girls and the rest office workers. When the signal was given, the prostitutes started to perform and undress.

The others just went along with the flow.

23

Larry I

The yellow twin-engine Cessna flew low over the ocean and up the beach toward the excavation project where the canals were being dug. Four draglines were dropping their buckets in and out, in and out, in and out. Larry sat in the copilot's seat with a stopwatch in his hand. "Twenty-two, twenty-three, twenty-four seconds for number one." He was timing how long it took for the bucket to complete its cycle, to come out of the water, pivot, drop its load on to the bank and return to the water and come out again. The weekly winner won a stainless steel wristwatch with plenty of little dials on it. Yes, it's the same Larry, the satyr, but he's thirty-five years old, still good looking and charming. Everyone working for Larry had been given a stopwatch as a gift. They had to wear them around their necks. They didn't realize it, but Larry had made them extremely time conscious. They were timing everything. They went crazy and even timed their pees. The production on the canal job was beyond projections and Larry was making big money in the Bahamas.

That night I had dinner with Larry at the casino. The casino manager treated us.

"Looeease, I'm gonna gamble."

That's how Larry enjoyed pronouncing my name.

He stood up and sauntered up to a private blackjack table.

"I'll play five hundred a card and take the whole table."

My eyes were popping out. He played six or seven hands all at once. There were three decks mixed into the cards and I had a feeling that, even so, he had memorized the action and had a jump on the house, but he drew at seventeen and went over. Then he "stuck" at seventeen and the dealer hit nineteen. He lost and he lost and he lost. He was down about a hundred and twenty-five thousand and turned to me.

"Looeease, please go get me five thousand in chips."

"Larry, I'm the attorney here. I can't gamble and I don't have an account."

"Looeease, poleese get me the chips."

" O.K. I'll try."

I walked quickly up to the cashiers' window.

"May I have five thousand dollars in chips please?"

The crisply dressed blond young lady looked at me.

"Yes sir, Mr. Ress. Do you still keep an account at The Second National Bank?"

"I do."

"Sign here. Here are your chips, sir."

I was quite surprised, and by the time it took me to write about it Larry had lost that five thousand too. That was enough. Larry was done gambling for the night.

Larry tipped the croupier and told him to have the loss charged to his account at the casino and we went into the bar for a drink. The bartender wouldn't dream of charging us. Larry didn't seem the slightest bit flustered He talked about the great weather we were having and the latest group of girls that he had met, but not one word about his losses. He told me that he was considering moving his three monster Manitowoc draglines up to Kentucky to do some strip mining. The mobilization cost, just moving them to Kentucky, was over three hundred thousand dollars. When we parted he said:

"Loooeeease, I'll have your mark cleared before you leave the island on Wednesday."

Now I knew two things: that I didn't have to concern myself about the chips and that I would be out of there by Wednesday. But as I tried to sleep I kept thinking how cool it was to be unconcerned about losing over one hundred and thirty thousand dollars in a few hours. Something just wasn't right. I had seen men much wealthier than Larry get aggravated over lesser amounts and especially with the idea of "losing." These men could not accept the concept of losing anything.

No, something was not right. Just as sleep was approaching it came to me. Didn't he say "Charge it on my account?" He had an account at the casino. The casino was owned by Bahamas Amusements Limited. Bahamas Amusements was owned by Great Bahama Island Enterprises. Larry was digging all of the canals for their residential development. They owed his company, E&B, Inc. well over three million dollars at a time, a good portion of which, the profits, was subject to American income taxes.

Larry was gambling with fifty-cent pre-tax dollars He could say: "Just take any losses on my account off what you owe me." If he won he pocketed the cash right at the casino, tax-free. There were no IRS agents in the Bahamas at that time. If he broke even he was in effect converting taxable money into tax-free money, saving fifty percent, at a cost of no greater than the six percent casino profit and being entertained as a big spender.

Do not tell me about Harvard graduates. They worked for him and Larry never finished high school.

I had a triple conflict of interest since we represented all of the entities involved, so I just kept quiet and made believe that I hadn't figured it out. It didn't take long for my former partner George Case, the president of Great Bahama Island Enterprises, to come to his own conclusions and Larry was no longer allowed to offset his casino account. It was great for Larry while it lasted.

Larry had moved the three Manitowoc giant crawler excavating machines to Kentucky, near Corbin. That meant getting permits to close roads all the way up from Fort Lauderdale. The cabs of these excavating giants were the size of a small house. I had looked at the contract before he signed to strip mine the side of a Kentucky mountain. It was winter when he negotiated the deal. He had gone on the property and also looked at it from the air. Of course it was winter and the snow was three feet deep. I warned Larry to make sure the subsoil conditions would support these huge machines. They weighed around eight thousand tons each.

We checked the seams that ran under the property, their depth, and the yardages which could be mined, and made sure that the contract protected him. The owner produced certified core borings confirming the soil structure and the coal quantity and quality. Sorting of the coal, transportation to rail cars and a contract to sell to electric utility companies were all in line. We were permitted and in compliance with the labor laws. Larry had no other use for the Manitowoc excavators at the time, so it was a smart deal.

I was concerned about dispute resolution in Kentucky, especially in rural Kentucky, so I inserted an Arbitration clause, providing for arbitration with the American Arbitration Association to keep us out of local politics. Kentucky did not allow arbitration in those days, but we had little to lose, and I believed that I would have a good chance to get the arbitration clause enforced.

It didn't take long for the phone to ring.

"Looeease, we got ourselves a big problem. The first Manitowoc has kept sinking into the ground. We get it straightened up and she crawls a bit and sinks in again."

"Larry, it sounds to me as if the property has been undermined, shaft mined."

"That can't be. I have the certificates of subsoil conditions and the core borings."

"You had better get the property core bored again. It sounds very fishy to me."

Two days later we learned that the engineers were unable to get core borings. The drill went down into vacant space. The property had been shaft mined and the tunnel entrances had been sealed and covered over with shrubs and obscured by the snow. The property was not strip mineable.

There was no point in trying to continue to dig. We made our claims and were met with the owner's lawsuit in the local state court. They claimed that the property was mineable, had the requisite yardage of quality coal and that we were in default. A quick check revealed that everyone up there was related. The judge was the attorney's cousin. The attorney was the owner's brother-in-law and the stench was terrific.

We had over three hundred thousand dollars in the mobilization costs alone. Then there were all the fees, labor charges, administrative costs and the lost projected profits. Our local attorney filed a motion to enforce the arbitration clause and it was summarily denied.

"Larry, I need the Lear jet for a day. I'm going to file for arbitration with the American Arbitration Association in Cincinnati and then fly to Little Rock to seek an emergency injunction against the Kentucky State Court. We will also ask the Court to enforce the arbitration clause under the Federal Arbitration Act."

My first stop was Corbin, Kentucky, where we filed a notice for Arbitration and a Motion to Stay Proceedings, along with copies of the petition, which we were filing in the Federal Court in Little Rock, Arkansas. Our local attorney was skeptical.

"I think you're going to trial here in Corbin."

The plane was waiting at the airport and we were off to Cincinnati. The copilot called ahead for a cab to the executive airport. When the taxi crossed over the bridge into Ohio I felt a sense of relief. Then the clerk at the American Arbitration Association office refused to accept our Arbitration Application.

"Kentucky does not permit arbitration. We cannot process your demand for arbitration."

I asked to speak to the office director. Again it became an argument. I finally explained that we were appealing to the Federal District Court for a ruling under the Federal Arbitration Act, which should prevail over Kentucky State law, to allow the arbitration, and that his office was the proper place to file. This would be a huge crack in the Kentucky prohibition of arbitration law and would open his office to a flood of arbitrations. There is a hefty charge for filing a multi-million dollar claim. The director was so convinced that we would be unsuccessful that he charged a token two hundred dollars. I walked away with certified copies of the filing of the Arbitration.

The jet landed in Little Rock. It was sunny and this time they had a limo to take me to the courthouse. My Petition for Emergency Ex Parte Hearing for an Injunction was accepted, along with all of the other documents. The judge was hearing a Motion, but I was allowed into the impressive courtroom. I never cease to be awed by Federal courtrooms. Two-story ceilings, polished wood benches, heavy draperies, thick carpeting and an elevated judge's podium, all the wood beautifully carved with American flags and eagles.

"Mr. Ress, what is this all about?"

"Your Honor, we are seeking an ultimate determination that the Federal Arbitration Act supersedes the Kentucky State law prohibiting arbitration. We are petitioning to Stay the Corbin Kentucky State Court from going forward in the pending lawsuit until this Court has an opportunity to consider and rule on our Motion to Compel Arbitration pursuant to the Federal Arbitration Act."

"Do you have a 'Proposed Order'?"

"Yes, Your Honor it's included in the file we have submitted."

"I see it. Granted. The clerk will advise as to the date of argument."

We had stopped the Kentucky Court from going forward.

The locals were being stirred up against the "outsiders." Larry's machines were being fired on by rifle shots from the woods. We suspected the owner's employees. Within a week we had a date to argue in Arkansas. Larry's plane was waiting for me. Special permission had been granted for me to appear as co-counsel with a local Little Rock attorney. The owner's attorneys from Corbin were there with local counsel, as was the owner, John Stensel, who turned out to be a grubby, heavyset roughneck.

It was three in the afternoon when we were called to the main courtroom to argue. My local guy was not presenting our case in a clear and distinct manner. He was making a convoluted argument and was being interrupted by the seller's attorneys at the end of every sentence. Finally the judge told them all to be quiet.

"Mr. Ress, You filed this petition. Explain what is going on here."

" Your Honor, this is a question of whether Federal Law prevails over conflicting State Law." (Federal judges like to hear that federal law prevails over state law).

I had his attention.

"My client contracted to dig coal in Kentucky to be loaded on to rail cars which ship it to Ohio, Arkansas and many other states. This very coal is used by various state utilities to produce electricity, which is on a nationwide grid. We are engaged in interstate commerce and this mining contract influences and is a part of interstate commerce. The contract specifically provides for arbitration of disputes with the American Arbitration Association and comes under the Federal Arbitration Act. We have filed with the American Arbitration Association. We are being sued in Kentucky and we respectfully ask that you determine that we are

164

entitled to arbitration and compel the Kentucky Court to honor and enforce any Arbitration Award which results from this arbitration."

Two days later the Federal Court ruled in our favor, and we were entitled to arbitrate. So back to Cincinnati for the appointment of an arbitrator. The American Arbitration Association manager was quite surprised. At a brief hearing, he selected Corbin as the place for the arbitration and named the arbitrator. When we got back to the office I looked up the arbitrator. The arbitrator's address seemed somewhat familiar to me. It was on the same street as Stensel's attorney. It was only two numbers different. Often attorneys have offices close to one another near the courthouse, but I had to investigate. Sure enough, they each occupied a side of a duplex with connecting doors. The arbitrator had been a former partner of the seller's attorney. They were still in a number of real estate deals together. Neither the attorney nor the named mediator disclosed this. Clearly the manager had appointed an arbitrator hand-picked by Stensel's attorney. Maybe the manager was bribed, or thinking of future sources of business, or was another country cousin, or was unhappy about the two hundred dollar filing fee—we'll never know, but he sure had to know what he was doing.

This time we demanded arbitration in Lexington and asked that the arbitrator be appointed from the official arbitrator's list, using a short list of three, each party having veto power until there was one arbitrator left. They agreed. We finally had an arbitrator. Now I found a Harvard Law School graduate, an older gentleman, but very sharp, to be lead counsel in Lexington Kentucky.

The arbitration came to a final hearing. We presented our claim. Stensel's lawyers produced experts who said that the property was not undermined and that, based on their engineer's borings, there was quality coal throughout the property, more than enough to satisfy the contract's gross requirements. Their engineer was a major firm in Atlanta, garlanded with Georgia Tech graduates. When we contacted them, they said that the studies were valid and done under their supervision, and that was their sworn testimony. Stensel, after numerous delays, had to produce his business records, which we received only after the first day of the hearings. That night, reviewing his cancelled checks I noticed a recent check paid to Billy Corbett of Kerrville, Texas, for three thousand dollars, without an explanation or memo on it.

Billy answered the phone at about nine o'clock at night.

"Oh, I had a feeling you might find me. I'm relieved. I can't be a party to a fraud. I'm a well driller here in Kerrville. Atlanta Engineering hired me to find coal on the Corbin property. I went out there and explained to Mr. Stensel that I was getting dry holes all over the place and that the property had been undermined. He said that there were columns which I should drill into and find coal. Each of the twenty positive borings I made throughout the property was obtained only after I probed to locate the columns that supported the roof of the excavation. All of the other sixty-two borings that went into empty caverns or dry holes were to be disregarded as though they didn't happen."

"No. I don't have a journal and nothing was in writing. Atlanta Engineering made out the report and told me not to submit an invoice. I'm embarrassed to tell you that I don't read or write, but I do remember every single hole that I drilled."

And he did. His testimony was devastating. He couldn't read or write but what a memory! He was able to describe any of the eighty-two holes that he had drilled including the date, the exact location and the results obtained. He diagrammed them on a large map. They couldn't shake him. He told of Atlanta Engineering and Stensel telling him to discard and forget about all of the dry holes. Atlanta Engineering had conspired with Stensel to try to defraud the arbitrator. Stensel had defrauded Larry. The award was over three million dollars against Stensel personally as well as his company for fraud. The Kentucky State Court reluctantly issued a judgment. We levied on whatever assets we could find, setting aside Stensel's evasive attempts to hide recent transfers and to create liens on his company's property, but there was still a large uncollectable balance.

Larry said to just write it off, but I was angry at Stensel, his attorneys and the conspiring "cousins" throughout the Kentucky-Ohio area, and I wasn't going away so fast. Stensel filed a personal bankruptcy. We countered that the arbitration award was non-dischargeable since it was based on fraud. The Bankruptcy Court ruled that judgment was not dischargeable.

Stensel came in for questioning as to his assets semi-annually. Our attorney in Little Rock, where Stensel lived, noticed that he was wearing a diamond studded Rolex.

"You can try a body execution here in Arkansas."

And we did. The sheriff stopped Stensel on the main street of Little Rock and impounded the Rolex, plus three hundred dollars in cash, and delivered it to the Federal Court Clerk. When Stensel and his attorney appeared in Federal Court to argue that the watch belonged to his wife who was a jeweler and that it was on consignment, the judge leaned over the bench and said:"I've never heard a worse liar and bullshitter."

It was a thirteen thousand dollar watch. I used the three hundred dollars cash to pay costs and gave the watch to our attorney as a gift.

Thereafter, once a year, every year, I brought Stensel in for questioning. He couldn't own anything in his name. He couldn't go into a business. I had him list his assets and produce his income taxes every year, even after Larry died. I renewed the judgment each time when it was about to expire. Before he died, Larry said:

"Enough is enough, Looeease. Let him go."

But I didn't think this lying, conniving bastard should get the best of Larry until, finally, after fifteen years, Stensel apologized and offered to raise some funds to settle. Larry's instructions were followed and the settlement became a charitable donation in Larry's memory.

24

Larry II

"I need you right now. Head up to the Fort Lauderdale executive airport. The plane will be waiting for you. I'm in Birmingham and I need you to get this deal I just made down in writing."

It was the phone at seven thirty a.m. I was already working.

Who else? It was Larry. It was to have been an office day, preparing for next week's trial. The file could be taken with me and reviewed while on the way to Birmingham. There was a phone on the plane. I would probably be back by nightfall. At any rate Larry was always appreciative and he always had interesting and challenging business transactions. I labeled him "Wild Larry," but never called him that to his face.

"Larry, we'll need secretarial help...typewriters, paper. Maybe you could use a local attorney. You won't need me."

"Looeease! Just get your pretty ass up here now."

This was another mining contract. It appears that there were very few Florida lawyers who knew anything about mining. Larry said that he trusted me, and because he did dredging, digging and mining I became self-taught, starting out by finding mining contract forms in law encyclopedias, graduating to specialized mining texts, progressing to the books on mining seams. Yes, the entire country's coal seams were charted and the type of coal and grade were usually described. I had created my own contract forms. Instead of accepting the standard forms, I made a list of all the clauses which should be covered in a mining contract. Compared to the formbook, my list had five additional clauses that they hadn't considered. I grabbed my mining form file and a handful of tapes, along with two portable dictating machines, which were the latest advancement in office technology, left word for my secretary and associate and drove to the airport. It was the same Lear jet waiting for me. As we reached thirty thousand feet the copilot offered the use of the airphone. My son Brad, eight years old, answered.

"Hey Brad, I'm calling you from six miles up in the sky."

"Dad, don't drink!"

Larry was waiting for me in a downtown hotel conference room, seated at a large table with five other men. They were smoking and appeared to be drinking bourbon. Larry introduced me. Each was the president of a corporation which either owned land or had mining rights to the land or was involved in Larry's deal. They seemed cordial and friendly. There were no other attorneys. They would represent themselves. They had significant contract and mining experience and they believed that this would be a pretty simple contract. O.K, but I knew better.

Larry escorted me into an adjacent room and outlined the transaction for me. In brief summary, his company would obtain the exclusive right to mine a large tract of land just outside of Birmingham. He had the legal description. The gentlemen in the other room had the mining rights. They had subterranean studies showing the extent of the coal and the quality. The coal would be graded by size by processing it through a sorter, a large, tall, compartmentalized bin. The land for the grader, the storage of the coal, and the assembly and parking and servicing of trucks would all be included. Trucks would be provided by a separate entity and the president was inside the other room. The roads to the railhead were owned and maintained by a different company and they would guaranty the safety and condition of the roads. The railhead belonged to the railroad and their representative was also sitting in the other room. They would provide the open coal cars, and the utility company would purchase the coal based on the price per ton for each grade shortly after it was delivered, as set forth in a separate exhibit. The contract was for the total production of the mine. Then there were the permits and compliance with all the licenses, labor laws, safety rules and multilevel regulations. Yeah—Really simple.

"Let's get started"

"Larry, where are the secretaries and the typewriters?"

"Looeease, right in this alcove…."

What? There they were: three hookers with long polished fingernails, low-cut blouses with their breasts popping out, heavy lipstick and rouge and mascara all over the place, and the sweet smell of cheap perfume. They had just finished servicing the five guys sitting inside and they couldn't even "hunt and peck" well. The typewriters were old stand-up Coronas and there was a stack of carbon paper. The girls were giggling and I was in a state of shock.

"Larry, we need to go to a local attorney's office to get this done."

"No way Looeease. It will take too long and I will lose this deal. It's very important to me to get this done here and now."

Think, Lewis. Think. What can I do? There must be some way.

I took out my dictating machine and inserted a tape. My yellow pad was out. Make an outline of the deal using my set clauses as a guide and add the specifics of this deal to them. I dictated the entire contract on the tape paragraph by paragraph, clause by clause, referring to each exhibit, carefully, slowly and distinctly. It took almost the entire tape. I played it back and made some corrections and ran back over it again. It would do. I brought the tape player into the main conference room.

"Larry, we're going to do a recorded contract. We'll all listen to it. I'll play it twice. Then each party can sign on the tape. I will recite that you have agreed to all of the terms set forth on the recording, and then ask you to each acknowledge, again, that you agree to the terms and are signing it electronically by stating your name, the name of your company and the words 'I accept and sign on behalf of …..' and state the name of your company. You will be signing by 'voiceprint'."

It was the creation of new law. I've never heard of anyone doing this either before or since. It was nuts, but it was working. There was no opposition. I was probably flirting with a malpractice suit and a Bar complaint, but maybe it would work. Can you have a taped contract in Alabama for mining land with huge sums involved and sign it by "voiceprint"? I wasn't even admitted to practice in Alabama. Maybe a clause that Florida contract law applies would cure that issue.

"Larry, order them lunch. Discuss how you are going to

implement the contract. Draw up schedules and timetables. Have the girls go back to work, but keep the men here. The contract will be back in four hours for re-signing."

Our best and fastest secretary, Joanne, was called to come by taxi to the Fort Lauderdale airport to meet the plane. She listened to the tape in my car on the way back to the office. She knocked off the contract in record time. My secretary prepared and attached the exhibits. The package was delivered back to the plane and was in Birmingham within hours, not four, but close to six. They were still there waiting, and it was signed by all, sealed and delivered in proper form.

We billed Larry twelve thousand dollars for twelve hours of work. In those days that was a big, big fee. Larry sent us a check for ten with a letter of appreciation. He mined the coal and everyone performed under the contract just as agreed. Larry made over two million dollars on that deal.

He said that the fee was very reasonable considering that, had he used a local firm, it would have taken a month and the fee would have ultimately been triple.

25

Larry III

The cruise ships used to tie up and the passengers would toss coins into the water. Nassau was changing. The harbor water wasn't crystal clear any more. The kids weren't able to dive for the coins. The straw market had become touristy. Bay Street was a hodgepodge of T-shirt and jewelry stores. Hog Island was now "Paradise Island," connected to the mainland by a toll bridge (now two toll bridges). The water taxis, small wooden boats, were mostly out of business. I ought to know about that first bridge. I drew all the documents for that bridge which went into effect at midnight and only a few knew who owned it. There had been a small casino in the Britannia Hotel where Howard Hughes had hidden out on the top floor. Now there's a second bridge and a gaudy new casino and a huge hotel with enormous fish tanks through which you can walk in underwater tunnels. You can plunge down high water chutes, tan yourself on private beaches, get massaged in the spa, and dine in glamorous restaurants. This is known as "Atlantis." Nassau will never be the same.

Another call from Larry had brought me "just for a few hours" over to the offices of a well-known Bay Street attorney to straighten out a few clauses in a contract Larry was signing. He was selling a large oceanfront parcel of property on Paradise Island. "We'll have you back home before ten o'clock tonight, Looeease." I had been picked up by the twin Cessna at four in the afternoon and was in the attorney's office by six.

The attorney's offices were upstairs, through a poorly lit narrow hallway over the tourist shops. The walls of the attorneys' hallways were covered with plaques describing the multiple corporations with supposed offices in that building, including banks, insurance companies, oil and gas groups, and many other international corporations. Actually, they were just mailing addresses or "drop boxes."

The buyer's attorneys were grouped around an old long wooden table with gold-trimmed high-backed chairs. A smaller chair at the end of the table was reserved for me. I noticed that I was sitting substantially lower than they, even considering that I am short. They literally had me looking up to them.

They handed me a contract of about fifty pages. They expected me to call Larry and have him sign it and then leave for Fort Lauderdale. Looking around the table, I introduced myself to the buyer's attorneys. There was Sir Lloyd Graves, the host, and to his right there was Canadian Counsel Mr. Herbert Myers of Toronto. On Sir Lloyd's left there was Mr. Harold Richman, the English solicitor. The buyer was a Canadian-English consortium. They planned on building a high-rise hotel on the property. The purchase price was eight million U.S. dollars.

Larry, probably based on his self-confidence and in an effort to save large attorneys' fees, had been representing himself until now. After all it was a relatively simple deal, his vacant lot for eight million. He suddenly realized that he was over his head. He knew that I represented the developer of Freeport and the owners of Paradise Island and that I was familiar with Bahamian real estate, so once more into the lion's den.

One glance at the first page of "representations and warranties" and it became clear that Larry was being hustled. They were making him the guarantor of their success and of their profits. The "re-zoning" and "construction plan approval" clauses had no place in what Larry described as a sale of vacant land in the "as is" condition. As I read on, the contract became more and more onerous. Larry was responsible for obtaining the building permits and access to the property for the construction vehicles and cranes.

"Gentlemen, I would like a little time to review your comprehensive contract. Can we adjourn for this evening?"

We agreed to meet at ten in the morning. Where was Larry? Certainly he was not at the airport to greet me. The pilot, Jeff, was waiting for me in the reception room.

"Larry asked me to have you room with me overnight. He's tied up right now and will get back to you."

Tied up? I found Larry at the roulette wheel in the Britannia Hotel with the sexiest woman I had seen in a long time. She was a blonde with green eyes, and wore a white low-cut sequenced gown, stiletto heels and a diamond necklace with a large matching emerald as the centerpiece. It matched her eyes. I won't bother to describe her figure, you have already imagined it. She was a knockout.

This was no ordinary lady. She was articulate and intelligent. As I explained the proposed contract to Larry over a drink, she paid attention and gently told Larry to listen to me. She was a

Columbia graduate with an MBA from the Wharton School and a very, very successful stockbroker with offices on Wall Street and an apartment overlooking the East River on Sutton Place. Larry was smitten with her and they were all over one another, touching, stroking, smiling, flirting and I had to get out of there.

"Larry, I need you tomorrow. I can't negotiate for you."

"Looeease, can't you see that I am busy. You take care of it."

I went back to the cheap room with the pilot, Jeff, and spent three hours going over one of the most one-sided contracts I had ever seen. Jeff had bought a toothbrush for me. The next morning I knew enough to buy the necessities, including a couple of shirts, socks and underclothes for two more days.

The three gentlemen facing me were brittle and formal. We went over each of their clauses. They had the advantage because we were working from their contract and not mine. At noon when we had time for lunch they would have the agreement redrafted and I had a chance to meet with Larry, who was in a lovely suite facing the ocean, with his lady friend wearing a silk robe, sitting up in the big bed.

"Larry, it's been a battle and they are being unreasonable. I don't like dealing with them. They are not trying to make a fair deal. They are trying to hustle you."

"Looeease, I know what you are saying, but I would like very much to make this deal happen. Compromise and try to get it done."

The amended contract, now fifty-two pages, was distributed. Wait a minute. The changes were not as we had agreed. There were three new paragraphs committing Larry to additional conditions. The compromises we had agreed upon were re-phrased to be unenforceable and meaningless.

"Gentlemen, it is apparent that your clients do not really wish to purchase this property because you have made this transaction impossible and unacceptable." It was eight o'clock at night and we were ending the second day of fruitless negotiations.

"I am tired and I am going to excuse myself."

We arranged to meet at ten the next morning. They would speak to their clients and get back to me.

It was the same routine. I reported back to Larry who was totally absorbed in wining, dining and gambling with his new girlfriend. He kept giving me words of encouragement.

"Looeease, you're getting closer."

It was Friday and evidently the terrible three had gotten instructions from their clients not to lose the deal, so they were a bit easier. However, each time we agreed to compromise, the document came back with words of different meaning. By Friday night I was ready to head home. Larry kept telling me that he wanted to sell this property and that he liked the price. The buyer's team kept playing unethical games. "Slippery" would be a kind word for their behavior.

I finally suggested that we dictate the changes to Sir Lloyd's secretary together. By eleven p.m. we had a contract, which had Larry not pressed me I would have never accepted, but he was making the ultimate decisions.

I met with Larry at midnight on Friday. He was gambling, but took time off to sit down with me.

"Larry, we've got a final draft and it's what you told me you could live with. I have to tell you something and get your instruction. These gentlemen haven't discussed a 'subsoil condition' clause. They've covered riparian rights (the ownership of land to the mean high-tide level on the beach) and they accepted our definition involving the median tidal water mark. They know about beach access to Bahamian water, but they haven't asked for a subsoil condition clause. I normally would suggest to them that they receive this protection, but they have been nasty and slippery and less than honorable and it's not your obligation to look after them. They have three lawyers to do that. The contract, at their insistence, says that it is fully inclusive and that there are no warranties or guaranties, oral or in other writings, except as expressly set forth in the contract. Do you know of any subsoil problems? No? Good. I certainly don't, but in any event I see no reason to look after them when they have been so nasty to us."

The contract was signed on Saturday morning and I returned home later that day. The three-hour trip on Wednesday had turned into an ordeal lasting three days.

About a month went by when Larry called.

"Looeease, they started construction. They drove pilings. The pilings disappeared. They drove more pilings. They also disappeared. They tried spread footings and the concrete disappeared. Quicksand! What do we do? They are claiming that the property can't be used for the purpose they purchased it and they want to overturn the contract and get damages."

"Larry, THEY put in the clause about no outside guaranties. They have no subsoil clause. They should lose in court."

If you haven't been in a Bahamian courtroom you should try it on your next Nassau vacation. It's a sight worth seeing. The Judge dresses with a full long wig, red robes and sits on an elevated "bench." The counselors wear full black robes, white collars and curly white wigs which they bring to court in big round hatboxes.

Frankly I wasn't used to seeing Bahamians in that setting and it was as though we were in a British High Court.

Our counselor was the prime minister's law partner. The judge asked a few pointed questions including who put the "limitation of guaranty and warranty" clause into the contract.

"They did."

And it was all over. Larry kept the eight million. I think that the property is still vacant.

He stopped dating the blonde. I wonder what happened to her.

26

Larry IV

"How are you fixed for cash? Do you have ten G's you can put up in a deal I have going?"

"Sure, Larry. What do you have in mind?"

"Looeease, I mean 'cash.' I've come up with a way of making cement from seawater. You know the canals I'm digging for George? Well I can build the seawalls for a lot less money than it would normally cost. I need cash to put this deal together."

It was a handshake and nothing else. I handed over an envelope with ten thousand dollars in cash and got a handshake. Larry didn't say anything else. Three months went by. It was known that Larry had landed the contract to build the seawalls and that they were going in and they were holding up as well or better than normal concrete. George told me as much. It was about one year later that Larry came up to me and said:

"Looeease, I'm making too much to share with you anymore. You're out. Here's your money."

The envelope was a little bulky, but I didn't look at it in Larry's presence. When I was alone I opened it. There was one hundred thousand dollars in cash. I guess I learned a little bit from my father, because I called my accountant and reported the profit and paid the taxes on it.

John Fordyce of "Fordyce and Simpson" had also been in the seawall deal. I wasn't aware of anyone else who had been involved, but it appears that there were some others. His partner, Jeri Simpson, was a crackerjack attorney and a rather sophisticated, mature lady. She was my friendly competition for the Grand Bahama Enterprises legal representation. She was extremely competent, well mannered, in fact refined, and was above any kind of petty behavior. We often worked together and were professionally friendly. She was in her late forties and a senior partner in the Fordyce firm. They had offices on Brickell Avenue, and represented a number of foreign governments. When you entered their large, plush office it was clear that the antique furniture was genuine. The walls were covered with elaborate documents confirming that they were the official representatives of countries like Malaysia, Thailand, and Singapore.

Jeri had apparently introduced John Fordyce to Larry.

Why John didn't declare the profit and pay the tax, I can only guess. It was tempting. Who would know? It was cash. Taxes were pretty high. At any rate he pocketed his profits. Larry was audited by the I.R.S. The deal was discovered and the government checked to make sure that all the profits had been reported. That's how they caught John Fordyce.

John was a highly respected attorney, fifty-five years old, Ivy League educated, "A-v" rated, with an unblemished reputation, the senior partner of a distinguished law firm with over thirty lawyers. The I.R.S. filed a criminal charge.

John went downstairs into his specially created wine cellar and hung himself.

More Larry

How does Larry get involved in my representing the Aetna Casualty Insurance Company? He does. Billy Jr., the son of one of the top state executives of the Aetna, had been struck by a car while walking across the street. Anyhow that's how it was presented to me. The driver said:

"He walked out right in front of me."

I undertook the case and met with Billy in South Miami Hospital. This was a nice, well-mannered young man, nineteen years old, who was clearly depressed. He had broken his left arm and his leg and both were in casts. He seemed unable to smile. My jokes were answered with a blank stare. There was little eye contact when he spoke and those few words or grunts were in a low deep monotone. He kept looking down. The hospital was first rate. Billy had a large, light, private room with plenty of flowers, but the nursing care left something to be desired, because the nurse did not come in once during my two-hour visit. I made several pages of notes, but I couldn't help but notice how "down" Billy was. What could I do? I knew Billy quite well and we had kidded one another and had a fun relationship in the past, sometimes telling dirty jokes. What could I do? I called Larry.

"Larry, this kid is really down in the dumps. Can you arrange for a lady to visit him?"

"Consider it done."

Billy was lying in his bed, staring at the ceiling when a very pretty twenty-two-year-old brunette with a stunning body came waltzing into his room carrying three red roses.

"Hello. Are you Billy? I'm here to deliver a kindness from a friend of yours."

With that she placed a chair against the door and dove under his sheets and administered a classic blowjob.

The next day Billy called and thanked me over and over again for the wonderful gift. He sounded happy. To my knowledge his father never found out.

Billy's case was settled for a considerable sum. I waived the fee.

It was about two months after the settlement that Billy did it again. This time he walked right out in front of a big truck. He didn't make it. Billy was dead at age nineteen.

* * * * *

Larry kept drinking and driving. He had me worried. Sooner or later we would be called to rescue him from drunk-driving charges. George Case had taught me the ropes of the D.U.I. (driving under the influence) defenses early in the game. We would use every strategy and technique that you could think of. The sobriety test was not performed exactly correctly. The machine had not been calibrated recently enough. The test machine had residue from a prior examination. Wiping it with alcohol to sterilize it before it was inserted into the vein contaminated the needle used to take the blood sample. The skin was wiped with alcohol, contaminating the needle as it took the blood sample. Our client was on a prescription cough medication and was unaware that it contained alcohol, confirmed by a helpful doctor. We had the case continued three or more times until the arresting officer failed to appear and then we moved for dismissal. When the client wasn't machine-tested it was easier. He or she had dizzy episodes from one condition or another like crystals in the inner ear or low blood sugar, all confirmed by medical testimony. We would worry about running out of excuses when we were called up for hearing before the same judge with the same client twice. Larry was a time bomb, ticking faster and faster.

"Larry, we can't help you out of this kind of trouble. They will throw you in a jail cell with ordinary criminals while you are waiting for us to bail you out. You are a target: rich, well dressed with an 'attitude'. The police will beat you up and charge you with resisting arrest. I have an idea. Why don't you rent a limo. It's a good way for you to conduct business with your clients in the back seat and do all the drinking you want. It will save you a fortune in the end and probably keep you out of jail. Also you're not a safe driver when you drink, and if you hurt a child you'll never forgive yourself."

That was it! The idea of hurting a child got to Larry. No more drunk-driving worries. Larry often made potential business deals in bars and the boys kept drinking into the night in the back of the limo.

On a Friday night at about midnight Larry and a business associate were drinking in the back seat when a twenty-three-year-old man driving a black pickup truck, and quite inebriated, went right through a stop sign and slammed into the passenger side of the limo at thirty-five miles an hour. The impact was like an explosion. It was heard three blocks away. The side of the limo where Larry was sitting was crushed. Larry wasn't wearing a seat belt. He was thrown across the back seat. His head was smashed against the opposite side of the limo. When we learned of the accident Larry was in intensive care and barely alive. The diagnosis was "fractured skull with severe trauma to the brain."

Larry was wrapped like a mummy. He had a vacant stare and didn't respond to my greeting

"Larry, if you hear me, blink your eyes."

No reaction.

"Larry if you understand me move your fingers."

No movement. He just stared straight ahead. Every few minutes he would groan. They were feeding him through a tube. There was no way to communicate with him. Maybe he would come around.

We filed guardianship papers and his staff took over business operations. Dick Halpert was the manager, a Harvard Law School graduate. Ken Doxtadder, known as "Mandrake with the books" (you may remember the comic strip "Mandrake the Magician"), handled the accounting and made the deposits, paid the bills and took care of the payroll. I visited Larry every other day mostly after work and then less and less frequently. He wasn't getting any better.

I made a call to my friend and client, Gary, a neurosurgeon.

"Gary, can you do me a favor and evaluate my friend Larry who has brain damage and is in Holy Cross Hospital?"

"Lewis you have strange ideas. I am not Larry's doctor. I don't have privileges at Holy Cross. If I touch him I can be sued and I put my license at risk."

"Gary, just do it will you?"

Two days later I heard from Gary.

"Lewis, your friend has extensive permanent brain damage. In my opinion he will not last a year."

Larry's wife and his girlfriend had a physical fight over him in the hospital room. Larry seemed to show some reaction when I told him that I had made a large charitable gift in his honor. His eyes moved, but he didn't blink or mumble and that was it. Larry died almost exactly one year after the accident. At the funeral I saw Christy, who had been Larry's sixteen-year-old live-in girl-friend. Larry had a fistfight with her father over her. She was now married to a good-looking fireman. We carried Larry's casket to the grave in a cemetery right on Route 84 in Fort Lauderdale. I drive past it all the time. As one of the three personal representatives appointed to handle Larry's estate, I learned that, aside from the double apartment on the beach next to the shipping channel at the port of Fort Lauderdale, he was worth only two million dollars.

Larry's three airplanes are long gone. Larry's lovely, lady-like wife got his money, remarried a neighbor who lived in the same building and moved to New York City. We went to the wedding. She was happy. Dick Halpert died shortly after Larry. Ken Doxtadder got Parkinson's disease and passed away about six months after Dick. Ronnie Blodgett took over the business, changed the name and since then two other companies have occupied Larry's office building and construction yard on Ravenswood Road. The last I heard his kids were living in a trailer park.

It's as though Larry never existed.

27

Slip or Trip

Floor maintenance is a true science. That's right. Under the United States federal government the Department of Labor has within it the Occupational Safety and Health Administration (OSHA), which publishes and enforces extensive rules and regulations for cleaning floors. Did you know that floors are not perfectly flat, and that liquid wax can puddle in a depression ever so slight and form a slippery surface, especially when wet? So floors must be scraped and then tested to make certain that the depth of the protective wax cover is not greater than the permitted amount. Did you ever hear of anyone checking the depth of their floor wax? Every commercial establishment must have a compliant floor-cleaning program, with regular daily inspection of the cleaning of the floors, carpets, steps and sidewalks, as well as accurate and complete written records of the inspection. If the coefficient of traction is not within the permitted range, or there is any other violation of a rule, the owner is liable for damages resulting from a slip and fall. This area of the law creates prime material for slip and fall attorneys because there usually is insurance coverage and therefore an open avenue for attorneys' fees. A good portion of the price of food in a supermarket includes insurance premiums for slip and fall coverage and supports a family of attorneys on both sides of the cases.

Wendy Vendenta, a buxom brunette, a single lady, age thirty-six, from New Jersey, had a bad fall at the Seaside Bar and Grill at the Holiday Hotel in Hollywood, Florida. She tore up her knee and had to have surgery at Broward General Hospital. The Seashore Bar was an open-air freestanding building right next to the pedestrian "boardwalk", directly on the beach. It was part of the huge old ten-story Holiday Hotel, which in turn had been the old Bible College which was earlier the old Hollywood Grand Hotel, going back to the nineteen thirties. She wasn't sure how it happened, but she noticed a banana on the floor after she fell. Her two girlfriends said that banana was on her shoe.

The insurance company wasn't paying anything and Wendy came to me for help. Was there really any banana on her shoe? The shoes had been thrown out. The witnesses, her friends, didn't see the actual fall or the banana, and surely didn't know how long it had been there, but they said that she suddenly slipped and then they saw the banana afterward and there was some banana on her sandal… sandals?

There was no talking to the insurance company adjuster. He told me frankly that they had marked the case for trial. There would be no settlement. He said that they were "loaded."

We filed a lawsuit and took a close look at those OSHA government-required cleaning records. They showed two inspections on the day of the accident. The first occurred at eight in the morning. The bar didn't open until eleven thirty. The second inspection showed no cleaning or flooring problem at ten in the evening. Of course that was after the accident, which happened at five in the late afternoon. There was no record of cleaning up a banana or anything else.

The accident report, which the insurance company required, didn't mention a banana and said that Wendy tripped on her own foot. It did however, show that there was a guest at the bar namely, a Valentino Brandon, from New Jersey, but there was no address and he had not been a registered guest at the hotel. No statement was taken from him and it appeared that he wanted nothing to do with the accident.

The two cleaning employees testified as they were obviously "prepared" to do. The bar's three other witnesses, its employees, were now working for the same employer, but in California. They each testified that they were present at the time of the accident and clearly saw Wendy trip on her own foot and fall down the two stairs that were next to the bar. All three saw her trip on her own foot: "I just happened to be looking at her feet as she walked down the stair and I saw her feet get tangled up. She tripped on the heel of her shoe. It was her right big toe striking the heel of her left foot."

Of course they had been coached. Insurance adjusters are trained in preparing the statements they want and having the employees sign them in the presence of the boss.

The banana case was developing quite a smell.

The case was set for trial. No offers to settle... My phone rings. It's a deep, clipped, very professional voice.

"Hello,.. Sir, my name is Valentino Brandon and I'm Chief of Police here in Long Branch, New Jersey. Your client's uncle, Frank Testa, contacted me about Wendy's case. Yes, I know about the accident. I was sitting at the bar on that day, on vacation and I saw the whole thing... I noticed the banana on the floor before she fell."

"....Yes, I actually saw her step on the skin and go down."

"Did I see the color of the banana?.... Yes. It was dark brown and black. It probably was on the ground a long time."

"....Yes, I'll be glad to give a deposition and I'll be in Florida for this year's vacation."

"Sign a sworn statement?... Of course. ... No, I'm glad to."

Chief Valentino Brandon signed a sworn statement which this time I prepared, and it was returned, notarized and accompanied by a covering letter on The City of Long Branch Police Department's stationery with the Captain's name engraved at the top in raised letters.

Case settled! Big bucks!

Wendy never told me that her uncle Frank Testa was also a police captain in New Brunswick, New Jersey.

Rotten bananas!

Courthouse Stairs

Ernesto Gonzalez had been practicing law in Miami for about a year. His client, Rosa Perez fell on the County Courthouse steps and suffered a fractured wrist and a back injury which resulted in about fifteen thousand dollars' worth of medical bills. She lost two months from her work as a real estate saleslady, and was unable to cook, clean and look after her husband and her young daughter. Her mother moved in to help Rosa.

Actually Ernesto couldn't find much to create liability.

There were two levels of a large outdoor plaza staircase covering the entire front of the building leading to the entry doors of the courthouse. This impressive white granite block structure had been built in 1924 and had been the tallest and grandest building in the entire South. It had tall Doric Greek columns and the first eleven stairs stopped at a lovely flat marble open area and then an additional eleven steps led to another large open area, then through the columns to the entry doors.

Rosa, wearing her low-heeled black pumps and dressed in a dark-blue skirt and white blouse, was on her way to file a real estate petition for tax relief. She had her small black leather purse and the petition in her right hand, and was talking to her best friend next to her about the location of the tax office. She was going up the courthouse stairs and was at the third or fourth step in the second level of stairs when suddenly she stumbled and went down hard. There was some screaming. Her left wrist was dislocated severely and she couldn't move her fingers. Her back was bruised and painful. A crowd gathered and the security police helped her up and supporting her under her arms, brought her into a small room inside the courthouse and sat her down until the ambulance came. She was crying.

Ernesto Gonzalez Esq. was a diligent lawyer. He had measured the steps and found that the third and fourth step, where Rosa had fallen, showed a rise up of eleven and one half inches while the other steps had only an eight-inch rise. Mr. Gonzalez argued at trial that all steps had to be in conformity with one another. His expert tried quoting the County building code, but he didn't have a copy of the 1924 building code and I stopped him cold.

The case went on for five days. I kept walking around the courtroom with a three-foot ruler, which the judge asked me to put away, but I kept bringing it out. No objections raised.

Final argument and Ernesto stressed the eleven-and-one-half-inch rise on the stair where the fall supposedly occurred and how our minds get tricked into thinking that the height of each stair would be the same as the preceding one.

My turn.

"Ladies and gentlemen of the jury I have been walking up and down the stairs of the courthouse every day and measuring them. They all differ in height to some degree, because our courthouse was built in 1924 and I sure don't want it torn down. It's beautiful. Thousands of people go up and down those stairs regularly without falling."

No one objected. The judge was squirming in his chair.

Out came the three-foot ruler and I laid it up against the platform on which the jury chairs were located. I measured it. The platform was fifteen inches high.

"Ladies and gentlemen of the jury, you have been going up to your seats on this platform and stepping back down to the courtroom floor at least five times a day for five days. You have stepped up fifteen inches, not eleven, and not one of you has tripped or fallen. Why?

Why? Because you pay attention to what you are doing. You look... and you step up and step down, thinking about what you are doing. The steps didn't cause this fall. The plaintiff wasn't paying attention to what she was doing...."

Verdict for the defense.

The Roxy Tumblers

The insurance industry had a research service that cross-indexed by name, social security number and the type of accident. As I recall it was called "The Index Bureau." They supplied you with small index cards which had information about the party claiming injury, including any prior claims, the type and location of the accident, doctors, hospitals, the name and address of their attorney and the injuries claimed. The bureau gave you the social security numbers of the claimants and the court case name and number.

The plaintiffs, Arthur and Betty Snyder, were seeking damages for significant injuries, including a dislocated shoulder, sustained when Betty fell down the stairs at the Doral Beach Hotel. There were six witnesses. They claimed that the carpet at the top of the stairs was wrinkled and bunched and not maintained in a safe condition, with no warnings of any type. Betty tripped on the rippled carpet and went down the eleven stairs, striking her head, neck, back, left shoulder and hands. The ambulance came and again, there were six independent witnesses. The accident report showed the defective rippled carpet, with photos to support the conclusion of negligent maintenance. The maintenance records, including the report from the night before the accident, didn't reveal any rippling in the carpet and didn't show in the reports until after the accident. The largest ripple or rise in the carpet was at least one inch high, just where the carpet met the start of the top stair.

After Betty was discharged from the emergency room with a diagnosis of "traumatic cerebral concussion with possible complications; shoulder separation, left; low-back syndrome;

multiple bruises... Patient prefers to seek her own physician," she went directly to the office of Bernard Berman, D.C., and a well-known local chiropractor who advertises heavily on billboards on the Interstate.

"Auto accident? Slip and Fall? In pain?
Let me be your doctor!
Berman and Associates, D.C.,
medical accident and pain management specialists. "

There were no associates.

Betty was outfitted with a sling, a cane, a Wallace Collar (circular neck brace), a low-back brace and was being separately treated for injuries to each of these areas two times a day, six days a week. The unpaid medical bills had passed the fifty thousand dollars' mark when the lawsuit was brought by Brown and Brawn, who also advertised by billboard on the Interstate, as well as on the internet. They also raised hefty sums of money for the re-election campaigns of many of the sitting judges and then tried cases before them.

"Injured in an auto accident? Slip, trip and fall?
Hurt at work?
You need help in collecting for all of your damages, including
pain and suffering.
We've collected millions for our injured clients.
I want to be your lawyer!
Bill Brawn..
Brown & Brawn and Associates, Attorneys"

It clearly was one of those built-up cases, and there was little you could do about it.

The Doral was insured with Texas Casualty, through the Small agency, which, in fact, was one of the biggest insurance agencies in the state. There was a basic five thousand dollar no-fault medical coverage which had been paid to Dr. Berman. The claims manager of the Doral, the insurance adjuster and I conferenced. Maybe we should pay the five hundred thousand dollar demand or at least make a substantial offer.

The Doral was "retro-rated," which means that their yearly claim losses, after a certain amount, were added to their future premiums. They had a lot to lose and didn't want to settle. The adjuster wanted to close his file and write the loss off in the current year. It was December. That's when a lot of cases get settled for internal accounting and tax reasons and because the claimants want Christmas money.

I was concerned with the treating doctor and the attorneys. They were both bad actors.

They had a slimy edge to them. Something didn't feel right. The most significant part of the claim, because it was objectively able to be seen and continued to be disabling, was the dislocated shoulder, which had never fully healed and was restricting Mrs. Snyder's activities and limiting her employment.

Betty Snyder was a skinny, tough-looking middle-aged lady with a small, sharp, protruding jaw, black-dyed hair, a lined chalk-colored face and a high pitched edge to her voice. She complained of headaches, but her attorneys produced no objective brain studies to back up this part of the case. They were only claiming a minimal permanent disability for the back sprain with no objective evidence of disability. Their main thrust was the dislocated shoulder, which severely limited Betty's activities.

We tried surveillance, but Mrs. Snyder was not driving and was holding her shoulder, rubbing her back and rubbing her head every time our cameras came near. She could spot a camera from a mile away. It was as though she had eyes in the back of her head. She engaged in no strenuous activity and went to the doctor's office regularly.

What about the Index Bureau? They showed the recent marriage of Mr. and Mrs. Snyder, their address and no claims.

"Let's try her maiden name." I was speaking to the Index Bureau in Atlanta. "It should be on the marriage certificate." And it was.

Her maiden name was Beatrice Adrionis, with an entirely different social security number. Born in Romania, previously employed by Sells-Gray Circus as an acrobat. There was a history of five prior accidents, two of which were tumbles. The first one down the steps of Radio City Music Hall, and the one only two years ago was down the steps of the Roxy Movie Theater in New York City, both due to rumpled carpet at the top step! She was known as "The Roxy Tumbler."

The elation at the Doral did not last long. The judge denied my Motion to Dismiss. I was in shock, too.

"Your Honor, these plaintiffs are professional, criminal, fraudulent staircase tumblers. They have a history of two recent identical claims where they were ultimately convicted of fraud and served six months in jail. Undoubtedly they created the rippled carpet and then tumbled down knowingly and intentionally in order to literally steal money…"

The judge spoke:

"Sir, you haven't proven anything related to this subject

claim. I'm not interested in what they may or may not have done in the past. These facts and this case stand on their own. She fell due to a dangerous condition on your client's premises. She suffered injuries, including a dislocated shoulder. You can attack her medical history, but you have an objective injury to the shoulder. You are speculating as to the accident itself and I don't buy it. Motion denied."

Back to the drawing board. I wasn't going to let this case get out of control.

Let's get her employment records. Sells and Gray, it turns out, went out of business in 1978, but the records were still around. We found them in a garage in Indiana. There they were. Beatrice was, in addition to being an acrobat, a contortionist known as the "Spider Lady" in the sideshow. She could put her head between her legs backwards and make her hands look like front legs and move just like a spider. In costume she was quite convincing. She was "loose jointed."

Let's get the medical records from the five accidents. Bingo! She had the same dislocated shoulder in each claim. We brought hr back in for another sworn deposition. This time she wasn't so tough. She evidently remembered those six months in jail. In return for an agreement not to file criminal charges, she admitted that she could voluntarily dislocate and then replace her shoulder back in its socket and that's exactly what she had done in our case after intentionally tumbling down the stairs. They withdrew the lawsuit with prejudice.

The judge seemed frustrated.

28

Psychopaths

Haulover Pier

"The judge wants you in his chambers immediately."

What is it now? It was the same judge who had recently ruled in my client's favor in a hotly contested workers' compensation case I had defended. The claimant had just lost her appeal. Maybe there was a loose end or two that the Court wanted to clean up.

As I parked my car in front of the Florida State Office Building it dawned on me that there might be more than a clerical problem, but what could it be? It was a clear, clean case and I had won it with convincing testimony. Hmm, what could it be?

"Sit down, Mr. Ress."

The Judge of Industrial Claims, Sam Mandel, looked out over his cluttered desk. There were about ten or twelve knick-knacks out there; a broken chess piece, some paperweights and a letter opener made out of a small military ammunition shell. Judge Mandel was a little overweight and balding, but he had once been a slim combat infantryman in the Battle of the Bulge. The Bronze Star was on the wall.

"Mr. Ress. You have a major problem. The claimant in the case you just won, Mrs. Frank, has filed a complaint against you. She says that you pushed her off the Haulover Beach Pier and that she fell twenty feet into the ocean. Her friend Mandy Fried signed a statement and says that she was there and saw the entire thing. It evidently was as a result of an argument you had with Mrs. Frank about her lying in her workers' compensation case. You met them on the pier, told Mrs. Frank that she was a damnable liar and then a pushing match started. You pushed Mrs. Frank over the rail. She has signed a Complaint and it's confirmed by her witness. I have it here. I'm about to refer it to the State's Attorneys' Office as well as the Florida Bar."

"Your Honor, that's insane. I've never even seen Mrs. Frank since the day the hearings were concluded. When did she say this occurred?"

"Here, it's right here. June 21st at three in the afternoon."

"Thank you Judge. This whole thing is a lie."

"She's got a witness and you had better be able to account for your time on June 21st."

I knew that it was a crazy woman trying to seek revenge, but what could I do? If I was out jogging or in the office, or driving my car, it might be tough to prove that I could not have been at the Haulover Pier on the 21st of June. The first thing was to look at my calendar. Believe it or not, I was in Jacksonville, four hundred miles away, on June 21st, negotiating with the Florida Special Disability Fund. My Eastern Airline ticket showed my arrival in Jacksonville at 8 a.m. and my return flight at 6:15 in the evening. Don Harrington, the fund administrator immediately sent me confirmation of our settlement discussions in

Jacksonville on June 21st lasting until 4:30 p.m.

Mrs. Frank never apologized and the Judge never charged her with anything.

* * * * *

Gladys

My friend, dentist and client, Buddy Krasne, owned a small office building in North Miami along with his brother, Alvin. They were the only truly honest dentists in the area. They didn't try to sell total mouth rehabilitation at five thousand dollars when the patient really just needed a few cavities filled. There were about five or six tenants in the building. One of the major tenants on the ground floor was Alfred May, an M.D. with a general practice. Dr. May was a little weird, but his wife, Gladys, was wacky. She would visit her husband's office daily and they would argue and yell at one another, disturbing the other tenants. Gladys would plop herself down on the floor in the hallway inside the building near the entrance and wouldn't get up. She would shout, sometimes scream. She was disheveled. Her hair was uncombed. She was unwashed and, above all, she clearly was stoned.

More than once, the Drs. Krasne had to call the police and have her removed. It was a few days after one of these events when the police served Buddy Krasne with a criminal complaint charging him with attempted manslaughter with a motor vehicle, and assault and battery with a vehicle, intentionally running over Gladys May.

The criminal complaint stated that Dr. Lawrence (Buddy) Krasne was driving his car in the parking lot behind the office building when Mrs. May came out of the building and was crossing the driveway in the back. It stated that Dr. Krasne, knowingly, maliciously and intentionally, drove his car into and over Mrs. May and after rolling over her, put his car in reverse and backed over her prone body in an attempt to kill her.

At first Dr. Krasne thought it was a joke and laughable. He called me and, sort of flippantly, said: "Lewis, please take care of this for me."

However, Dr. Krasne soon learned that it wasn't a joke and that it would be his word against that of Gladys May. The case was assigned to Judge Henry Balaban. Buddy played tennis with the judge and the judge immediately disqualified himself. The next judge was George Schultz, who was a friend of the Krasne brothers. He also recused himself. Next was Judge Milton Friedman who was also a friend, so he was out.

It was so ludicrous that each one of the judges had to get a joke or a jab at Buddy.

"Buddy, you really should drive more carefully and stop trying to kill your tenants." That was George Shultz. Judge Balaban also got in a jab.

"Buddy, How could you do something so terrible?"

We finally had a judge who didn't know Buddy. I started to worry about this case. Buddy was a kind, happy fellow and he would make jokes and kid around. Gladys May was nuts and could say anything. She had been a mistress of Diego Rivera and he had painted her portrait in oils. She was weird, wild, bombed half the time, and totally unpredictable.

As is turns out Buddy was in fact actually in the parking lot driving his car at the time and Gladys May was in the same parking lot at the same time. Her husband, Alfred May, who was also weird, had been treating her for a tendon tear and dislocation of her right shoulder, which, they claimed, was related to the assault, and she had a sling on her right arm and shoulder. She produced clothes that were dirty and grimy and claimed the dirt came from the surface of the parking lot. Dr. Krasne had of course denied the entire event.

I could also see a negligence case for punitive damages coming at us.

The case went to a non-jury preliminary hearing and my associate, secretary and I accompanied Dr. Krasne to the courtroom. I was more worried about the outcome than he. I think it was dawning on him that this was not a joke. Gladys appeared looking a bit glazy-eyed and eventually, with slurred speech, told her story. I cross-examined her and noticed that she was wearing her sling on the left arm and shoulder and not the right arm.

"Mrs. May, I thought you injured your right arm and shoulder, yet you are wearing your sling on your left arm and shoulder."

"Oh, I just forgot this morning and put it on the wrong arm."

Case dismissed. Buddy Krasne loves me.

In the Name of God.

My client was in the restaurant-supply business in New York City and had sold John and Mary Martin fifty thousand dollars' worth of used equipment, which John had shipped, to Miami when he started their restaurant. John had paid the notes securing the balance of thirty thousand down to ten thousand dollars and then defaulted when the restaurant went under, as so many new restaurants tend to do. My client, Acme Restaurant Supply Co., had written the ten thousand dollars off, but was attempting to salvage anything they could from Mr. and Mrs. Martin.

After getting no response to my letters suggesting a workout, I filed suit on the notes and for attorneys' fees and costs. The Martins didn't appear or contest the suit. So I obtained a judgment for ten thousand dollars plus two thousand dollars in fees and two hundred and fifty dollars in costs. When I finally contacted Mr. Martin he was quite street-tough.

"I went down and I have nothing to pay Acme back with. They can afford to take the loss. They can go take a leap. You'll get nothing from me, or my wife. We have no assets. You're wasting your time. Stop bothering us."

I didn't like the guy. He was a smartass, but he was right. I could find no assets upon which to levy. They were judgment-proof. I recorded the judgment with the County Clerk and waited.

About three or four months later I was scanning the *Daily Law Review* for new lawsuits filed and, lo and behold, John and Mary Martin had filed a lawsuit for injuries sustained by Mrs. Martin in an auto accident. Copies of the lawsuit showed the names of their attorney and counsel for the insurance company. The defense lawyer had no love for Mr. and Mrs. Martin and as the case progressed he kept me updated. When the case was settled for twenty thousand dollars he told me when the check would be sent to the Martins' lawyer. I had the Sheriff levy on their attorneys' trust bank account and the Court froze all of the settlement funds including their attorney's fee.

Mr. Martin appeared in my office and dropped to his knees in front of my desk.

"Mr. Ress, Sir, I beg you in God's name! My wife is injured and needs the settlement money to pay her medical bills. My lawyer is threatening to sue me. Please, please I promise. In God's name I promise and swear to make all of the payments. I swear in God's name that I will pay everything. Please help me."

There were two phone calls to make. The first was to Acme. They said that they had written the entire balance off their taxes and preferred not to show the income and to do whatever I wanted. They would be thrilled to get half.

Then a call to the rabbi.

"Rabbi Wallach, this man is invoking God's name and asking for mercy, but I don't believe him. He is a mean, bad guy."

"Lewis, if he's invoking God's name you must have faith that he will keep his word."

I went back into my office and spoke to Mr. Martin.

"You owe thirteen thousand dollars all told. This includes some interest. I will release six thousand five hundred dollars from the levy on your attorney's trust account and I will keep an equal amount, but you must sign a note and keep your promise to pay the balance. I have gone out on a limb for you. The only reason we are willing to do this is that you invoked God's name and have sworn to pay back the six thousand five hundred dollar balance in six equal monthly payments."

"I swear I will."

I never heard from John Martin again.

29

The Parkland Deal

A group, mainly doctors, was buying two thousand acres of land in the City of Parkland in west Broward County. It was un-platted raw acreage. It had been a sod farm, used to grow Saint Augustine grass. The grass would be strip-harvested and new grass grown on the rich topsoil of muck until the entire topsoil was exhausted and you were down to rock. Then the farmers sold what they thought was barren, useless land to the city slickers. However, civilization had crept out to the sod farms at the edges of Broward County, and the property would soon be ready for houses. There were no roads into the property. Ed Trumpet, the plastic surgeon, had found the deal through a friendship with an-other doctor, Samuel Paul, and Ed had brought in Kenny Lustig, the neurosurgeon, as co-trustee. Ed and Ken were to be compen-sated at two percent of the total sale price when the property was sold. Both Ed and Kenny were friends and clients of mine. The original purchase price was nine hundred dollars an acre, or one point eight million, with a ten percent down payment. The trust agreement provided for the trustees to actively market the prop-erty and described the voting procedure for approval of a sale. I was offered a participation of one and one half percent for twenty-seven thousand dollars. It was allowable at that time.

The trustees listed the property with Holland Realty and within two years an offer was received at a price of seven thousand two hundred dollars an acre with twenty percent down and a mortgage for the balance.

Yes. Yes! Over fourteen million dollars, almost eight times the original price. The purchasers were the Prosser family, the richest Jewish family in the United States. They owned vast amounts of real estate, office buildings and a major hotel chain. They even had a medical school and a law school named after them. Their local attorney, Martin Borkin, was a Yale Law School graduate and very experienced.

The deal was accepted and we exchanged the appropriate documents at the closing. The Prossers were not present.

Ed and Ken received their trustee compensation of two percent of the down payment and monthly trustee checks as the mortgage payments came in. The Prossers made payments for about a year without asking for a partial release of land and then suddenly, nothing. Telephone calls to Martin Borkin went unanswered. Finally he responded. He couldn't explain why his clients weren't making their mortgage payments and suggested we contact the Prossers directly. The Prossers' Chicago attorney responded. It was a clipped conversation. He told us that they were well aware that they had defaulted under the mortgage. He said nothing else. A number of participants in our group called me.

"Where's my check for this month?"

"Why don't we just foreclose?"

The trustees asked the same question. Well, one doesn't just foreclose against the Prossers. It means filing a lawsuit against them; naming them as a party defendant; saying that they defaulted under an obligation; filing in the public records. No. No. One just doesn't do that.

"Ed, you and I should go to Chicago and talk to the Prosser family before we do anything else."

"Lewis, what do you expect to accomplish?"

"We don't have a choice. We have to sit down with them and treat them in a refined manner. We can always sue. Why make enemies of the Prossers?"

We were invited to meet with the Prosser family for lunch. I went up the day before and did some scouting. The Prosser family had their own high-rise office building in downtown Chicago, with offices on the penthouse floor. They were a tight family group of brothers and cousins and uncles. Each participated in making family decisions with a majority ruling. Their attorney indicated that he was not required to attend the meeting. It would be hard to get them to reverse a decision. They had arranged for me to have privileges at their private club for dinner. It was a very formal, intimate lounge and restaurant with dark-brown leather furniture, low lights and servants appearing out of nowhere to offer drinks and pick up your glass.

There was a rather loud group in the back room and Anita Greenberg moved away from them. She came towards me. Her blue eyes twinkled. Her blond hair caught the light. She was a sexy lady with a very low-cut red dress... and she was pretty much bombed. She was recently divorced from my dental friend, Harvey. She put her arms around me and said that she couldn't believe that she would find me here. She didn't explain what she was doing over two thousand miles from home. One of the men called her to come back into their room and she let loose with a stream of cursing that I had rarely, if ever, heard from a woman. She was evidently one of those ladies who couldn't hold her booze and became ugly. The next time I saw her in Miami she was quiet, well mannered and merely mentioned how delightful it was to run into me in Chicago.

The next morning Ed Trumpet arrived right on time and we went up the glass elevator to the penthouse floor. The Prossers had their own small private dining room. It was kosher food and a little old short Jewish lady with an apron tied high on her chest served us chicken soup. The Prosser family was all there. They were plainly dressed in inexpensive white shirts, probably from Costco, tan slacks and brown sweaters, Timex watches and no jewelry. You never would have guessed their wealth and importance.

No business was discussed during the simple meal, which featured boiled beef. Afterward we met in their conference room, all glassed-in, facing the lake and the skyscrapers of Chicago. The table accommodated at least twenty people, but there was only Dr. Trumpet and me in our suits and ties, and "Uncle Jack" Prosser in a tan cardigan sweater. He got right down to business.

"Lewis, of course we knew what we were doing when we defaulted. Go ahead and foreclose. Better still, we'll deed back the property to you in lieu of foreclosure."

"Mr. Prosser, in all due respect, we came up here to talk to you about reinstating the mortgage without charging any penalties or fees. We don't want to lose this sale. There are numbers of widows and older retired investors who need to rely on this mortgage interest income."

"Lewis, please, we have considered that economically it is impossible for us to develop this land at a profit. Here's paper and pen. You 'push the pencil' and show me how we can do it."

" Mr. Prosser I am not as knowledgeable or as experienced or as successful as you, and certainly would not be in a position to question your business judgment. All we ask is that you reconsider."

"Mr. Ress, Dr. Trumpet, we've had a vote and made up our minds to abandon this project. You can have a deed back."

"Mr. Prosser, you know that we represent many investors and have no choice but to seek a deficiency judgment in a foreclosure which will amount to over three hundred and fifty thousand dollars. Can we negotiate a compromised amount?"(Was that **me** talking to one of the richest men in the world?)

Uncle Jack looked at me slowly, without any anger and actually wished me good luck.

"Our very qualified attorneys both here in Chicago and in Florida tell us that in Florida, when a seller takes back a purchase money mortgage which is part of the financing of a sale, there is no entitlement to a deficiency judgment and we must follow the advice of our attorneys."

"In all due respect, I don't agree with that conclusion. Is it alright if I send you the lawsuit in the mail without having the Sheriff serve it? We truly dislike filing this foreclosure, but we have to protect our investors."

The judge ruled that we were entitled to a three hundred and fifty thousand dollar deficiency judgment, which really represented a loss of profits. My fee was on a contingent basis and came to one hundred and seventeen thousand dollars, plus I had a delightful dinner at the Prossers' club and their local attorney, Martin Borkin, became a friendly acquaintance of mine.

So now we had the two thousand acres back. I knew that Ed Trumpet got this original deal from Dr. Samuel Paul, a proctologist who specialized in rectal surgery. A skinny guy with a mean look, more like a scowl, Dr. Paul was a real estate buff and had acquired a large tract of about four thousand acres. He had sold off half, or two thousand acres, through Dr. Trumpet, to his fellow physicians, supposedly at the same price per acre that he had paid. Everyone was grateful to Dr. Paul.

Dr. Trumpet now received a non-negotiable offer of nine thousand dollars an acre from a corporate buyer, Interco Inc., who we were told was also going to buy out Dr. Paul at the same price per acre. Ten percent was to be paid at the time of closing, the balance to be paid in a long-term low-interest mortgage. It sounded like a good deal. Dr. Paul contacted Ed Trumpet and was enthusiastic. A tenfold profit! … and we would keep all the payments previously made by the Prossers. Dr. Trumpet and I were still a little skeptical. Land prices had been rising. Parkland now had a residential subdivision not too far from our property. Zenith, a large international corporation was building an entire City of Coral Springs only a few miles from us. Interco required, as a condition to the deal, total written acceptance by all members of our group and in addition, a release to Dr. Paul to be signed by each of our members.

Our group was too elated to worry about these details, but Ed and I were concerned. Why would a corporate purchaser insist on individual releases for Dr. Paul? Our investors really didn't care, except for two.

The contract required one hundred percent approval and we had two partners who wouldn't sign. They were concerned about Dr. Paul's integrity and why he, through Interco, would insist on individual releases. They asked me to get to the truth. Neither Dr. Paul nor Interco would discuss the terms. We were told to just accept or reject the deal. The objecting partners directed me to sue.

We slid into some vicious litigation which revealed that Dr. Paul had been approached by Interco, who intended to make an offer for the entire property, Dr. Paul's and ours, at fourteen thousand dollars an acre. Dr. Paul told the buyer that the contract was to be realigned and split so that he, Dr. Paul, would get nineteen thousand per acre for his property and our group would only get nine thousand dollars per acre.

We sued Dr. Paul for fraud. Dr. Paul's famous lawyer, Waldo Gray, the grandson of a famous Supreme Court Justice, was as nasty and devious and slimy as Dr. Paul, but the facts came out from the buyer's executives. Interco, sensing that it would be facing a claim for collusion and conspiring to commit fraud, withdrew the offer, but Dr. Paul had to pay some very serious damages and everyone found out what a schemer and scoundrel he was. To Dr. Trumpet he became a mortal enemy.

The property was back on the market.

* * * * *

Dr. Paul died, a much maligned and disrespected person. His own family rejected him and he was entombed alone in a mausoleum. Dr. Trumpet had been making arrangements for his own funeral and, having divorced his wife, he was looking for a space in a mausoleum. The cemetery told Dr. Trumpet that they had a marvelous spot for him and Dr. Trumpet bought the remainder of placcs in the mausoleum with the one person already resting there. Only much later did he learn that it was Dr. Paul.

They would rest side by side forever. Or would they?

Gerhardt Gunderson called. He was the president of Zenith of Florida. He had a heavy Scandinavian accent.

"Mr. Ress, I would like to talk to you about your client's property in Parkland."

"Certainly, but if it is to acquire the property you should be talking to Dr. Trumpet or Dr. Lustig, the co-trustees."

"I know just what I am doing, sir. I wish to speak to you. It is a personal matter. Can you visit with me at my office in Coral Springs?"

We made an appointment and I was invited into what appeared to be a small two-story ballroom with a polished black marble desk the size of a large conference table. Mr. Gunderson's hair was styled. He was manicured. He was wearing a double-breasted Armani. The shirt was Ascot Chang with Bulgari cufflinks. I couldn't see his shoes. There was no doubt that he ran the show for Zenith.

"We are, in fact, interested in acquiring your client's property, but I will not have direct dealings with them, particularly Dr. Trumpet. Amongst other things he is known as a deal killer. He believes that no matter what offer may be made, it is insufficient because the buyer would never make a purchase unless it was able to make a significant profit and therefore the property is always worth more than any offer. I will not negotiate with that mentality. We know who you are and we will not negotiate with anyone else but you."

"If I may, Mr. Gunderson, I will advise my clients and get back to you."

Dr. Trumpet was not amused. He stated that he personally did not want to sell his share at this point in time for tax reasons. He instructed me not to negotiate or even pass any offer on to him or Dr. Lustig. The property was not for sale at this time.

"Ed, you are a 'trustee for compensation.' There is no higher duty under the law. You have an obligation to actively seek buyers not just to communicate offers, but also to actively promote the sale of the property. There are widows and older retired doctors who have good reason to want to sell the property right now while they are still alive and have a great need for money. You cannot do what is best for you personally at their expense. You are getting compensation for this."

"Lewis, don't tell me what my obligations are. You will do as I instruct. As a matter of fact, you are fired!"

Dr. Lustig was not happy with Dr. Trumpet's action.

"Lewis, you are NOT fired. I am a co-trustee and I say that you are to seek an offer from Zenith which I will pass on to the investors. Also, I personally am interested in selling."

When Mr. Gunderson agreed to come to my office, I knew that Zenith had a sincere interest in acquiring our property. We talked price and terms. He knew that the last buyer had walked away from a fourteen thousand dollar an acre offer and he stated that after pressuring his board Zenith would match that deal, but only with a long-term low-interest mortgage and with the condition that we cooperate and that, together, but at our expense, we obtain re-zoning of the property to a minimum of two houses per acre, with some commercial lots to service the community. We would be required to accept Zenith's development plan and release lots from the mortgage as they selected at the same rate per acre as they paid for the property. The closing would be held up until the re-zoning was complete

Negotiating is an entirely different animal than transmitting offers and drawing agreements. If you push too hard the buyer may take a walk. If you don't press for your terms the client, and in this case I was a part owner, suffers. If you take too long the buyer may lose interest or have financial reasons to withdraw. If you push too hard they may think that you are anxious and refuse to budge.

Dr. Trumpet wouldn't even talk to me. He had hired Robert Lowenstein, the husband of one of his major plastic surgery patients, to represent him. Ed had "redone" Mrs. Lowenstein from her scalp to her toes. She was a great source of business, recommending him to everyone who would listen.

Lowenstein told Ed that a trustee didn't have to seek the sale of the property, and didn't even have to transmit offers. Lowenstein told him anything Dr. Trumpet wanted to hear, including that not only was I wrong, but that I was a disloyal ingrate. This was Lowenstein's tactic, to turn Dr. Trumpet against me and, at all costs, to prevent Dr. Trumpet, Dr. Lustig and me from reconciling, and he worked at it. Trumpet and Lowenstein refused to have dinner with Lustig and me to discuss a resolution of our positions. Ed wouldn't talk to me. My relationship with my friend, Dr. Trumpet, was never the same.

Dr. Lustig could smell litigation in the wind and told me to negotiate on my own.

Mr. Gunderson seemed reluctant to negotiate, even though we weren't about to re-zone the property to Zenith's specifications without plenty of cash being irrevocably paid at a closing.

It seems that good luck finds me when I am most in need because a call came in on my private line, with the caller saying that it was a confidential call about the Zenith deal and asking if it was a secure phone.

"I am a manager with Zenith and loyal to my company. I have a family here in Coral Springs and I have reason to want Zenith to purchase your client's property. I want to stay here in the Parkland area where my children are in school and have friends and not move to the West Coast. Within reason, I will help you make this deal, but you must never reveal that you are receiving information from me. Promise that you will never try to find out who I am and that, if you do, that you will never reveal it to anyone."

It made sense. It could take thirty years to complete the development of our land.

"I promise."

It might be a trick of Gunderson's, but in any event I wasn't going to take less than a price which I had already set in my mind. It couldn't hurt as long as it wasn't illegal. I would ask nothing, but only listen.

"Gunderson acts tough, but they really want your property. They'll pay a good bit more and you can eliminate any conditions that make the deal contingent. You can safely ask for twenty-five thousand an acre and they won't blink an eye. I'll call you again."

And so it went, back and forth, with phone calls from my anonymous source.

Zenith was up to seventeen thousand an acre, with only a cooperation clause for the re-zoning, which would occur only after the closing. Mortgage releases would be at one hundred and twenty-five percent of the price per acre, and the released parcels had to be connected along a contiguous property border to avoid "checkerboarding."

The remaining issues were that they wanted us to approve their development plan sight unseen. The interest rate on the mortgage was two percentage points too low. They were only putting down ten percent and using a dummy company to buy the property so that they could walk away without any consequences and we would be stuck with released parcels.

It would take fifty more pages to fully describe the ongoing give-and-take sessions. Zenith was intentionally dragging out the negotiations. My inside advisor kept encouraging me. I was down to twenty two thousand an acre. They were at eighteen.

"They will pay more, but they won't make Zenith liable on the mortgage note."

I called Gunderson.

"Mr. Gunderson, I have full authority to negotiate, but I have to sell this deal to the investors and Dr. Trumpet is out to kill this no matter what it takes. In one final effort, we will split the difference in price at twenty thousand an acre, but it has to be all cash. In that way I don't have to concern myself about mortgage terms, interest, releases, re-zoning and other issues which would just make it very difficult to explain and thus to sell to our investors."

"I'm sorry Mr. Ress. Zenith has gone as far as it can go."

Back to my office. It looks like "no deal." The phone rang.

"Stick to your guns. Twenty thousand an acre, all cash. Gunderson is just about to receive an accounting report showing that we have more than enough cash to make the deal, and the home office in Pittsburgh is, according to my friends there, about to instruct him to make the deal."

Two days later Mr. Gunderson called.

"Draw the papers. We have an agreement. Now you get it approved by your group."

Twenty thousand an acre all cash wasn't hard to sell despite Dr. Trumpet telling everyone who would listen that the property was worth more.

Kenny Lustig proposed that I be paid one hundred and seventy-five thousand dollars in recognition of my negotiating efforts in addition to my legal fee. Forty-nine percent of the group approved, but Harry Kantor, my children's pediatrician and who I knew quite well, held the deciding two percent and wouldn't go along because of pressure from an eye doctor who sent him patients. The eye doctor, who just happened to hate all lawyers except his own, was bending to pressure from Dr. Trumpet. No special fee for me.

Kenny then paid me a one hundred and thirty-five thousand dollar fee for handling the closing. I also owned one and one half percent of the entire deal, which came to an additional profit of five hundred and seventy thousand dollars.

Years later, but only recently, Harry Kantor called a couple of my friends and thanked them profusely for hosting him at a lovely dinner party. He didn't seem upset when they told him that the dinner party hadn't occurred yet, but was next week. Then he forgot to show up.

Robert Lowenstein, that conniving son of a bitch, was the first to die. I don't celebrate anyone's death, but I didn't grieve.

Dr. Trumpet sold off the units he held in the "Paul mausoleum" and was placed in his own vault. I was at the funeral. Ed suffered complications when they inserted a shunt into his skull to relieve pressure on the brain. He degenerated over three years to the point where he couldn't recognize anyone, couldn't talk and ultimately had to be fed through a tube. When he could somewhat function he seemed to be friendly to me. He really was a very dear old friend, an extremely intelligent man who volunteered to help the wounded in Israel, raised funds for the hospital there, formed a successful hospital here and was a very highly regarded plastic surgeon. He subscribed to a tax service and knew more tax law than many of the tax lawyers. Parkland in great part caused us to lose our close friendship. Frankly, it wasn't worth it.

Kenny Lustig knew that it was coming. He had an inherited cancer problem, which had caused him to lose an eye early in life. He was a very cool, formal, one-eyed brain surgeon, probably the only one in the world. He also had many sophisticated interests, including collections of fine rugs, oil paintings and stamps. We were very close. He hugged me. He would never discuss his vision with anyone else. He was somewhat staid, like all neurosurgeons. Over fifty percent of their patients die while under treatment. He had impeccable training at Johns Hopkins medical school and was accepted there as a neurosurgical fellow. He asked me if his false eye matched. He spent the last thirty days of his life visiting me sipping coffee almost every morning. He kept hugging me. He's buried right near my parents. It's the same cemetery where Ed Trumpet is. I visit often.

Parkland is now a thriving city. The beautiful homes that we bargained about have been built. Maybe there is one person who moved into Parkland who knows the real story of how the property came to be developed. His kids are most likely finished with college and he's ready to retire from Zenith.

30

The PACE Bank:
"PACE, the friendly place"

The PACE Bank was located at the junction of Alton Road and the southwest corner of Fifth Street in South Beach. The bank was on the corner. The building entrance was cut off on an angle and the diagonal opening had automatic sliding glass doors controlled by sensors at the sides of the doors so that they opened and shut as customers approached and then entered the bank. The large sign read:

"PACE, the friendly place."

Annette Arnold was ninety-two years old and not a trouble-maker. She lived by herself in a small apartment on Miami Beach and was almost totally self-sufficient. They sent a helper to do the wash, change the sheets and do the heavy work once a week. Annette was white-haired, frail, weighed about ninety-five pounds and walked slowly with a cane, but she got around. On this particular clear, dry day in September she walked two blocks to the bank in order to withdraw some money. She says that as she entered the bank the automatic doors opened and then as she was going through, the doors slammed shut on her knocking her to the ground, fracturing her right hip.

The ambulance came and took her to Mount Sinai hospital. The bank made out a report and at least five employees said that as she crossed the entrance threshold she tripped on her own foot and fell. Their statements were taken on the day of the accident and photographs of the scene with the witnesses pointing to the place where Annette fell were in the file.

Under Florida law there was little to claim. Annette's medical bills were covered by Medicare. She wasn't working so there was no lost income and her pain, suffering and any disabling injuries would only be covered during her life expectancy, which was probably measured in months rather than years. Then there was lousy liability. The witnesses were numerous, a mix of women and men, young, smart and even a little sharp. Annette had no one. It was her word against the bank's five employees and she was a bit senile.

Marty Swift, a South Beach attorney against whom I had litigated in the past, had called and asked me to take on the case. The bank and its insurance carrier would pay nothing. Nada. Zip. It was a tough situation with no rainbow at the end of the trail. I felt sorry for Annette. She was alone in this world. No husband, and two children living in New York who didn't visit more than once a year.

Marty took me over to the nursing home in North Miami to meet Annette. What a putrid experience. The place was stinking from urine, feces and vomit. The beds were in a ward, about ten to a room. The moaning and groaning and screaming and crying were unrelenting. It was living hell. Annette was cogent and smiled and apologized for bringing me there. She was using a walker. Her face was deeply lined. Her eyes were dim, as though they were covered by a membrane. She spoke softly, but she described the accident very clearly. I thought that she was telling the truth. If so, the famous model bank and its employees were the biggest liars and some of the most dishonest people on this earth.

There was only one place to start. File a lawsuit... and I did. We started circling one another like two contenders in the boxing ring. The insurance company attorneys were one of the nastiest law firms in town. I was certain that they were bigots. They were just mean, unfriendly, unreasonable bastards. I took seven depositions in one day. Each of the bank's employees stood strong. They were told to be safety conscious so they paid attention to the elderly when these folks walked through the door. Each one swore that Annette tripped on her own foot and fell, flinging the cane to her right. Then there was the president of the bank. Everyone in the entire county knew him He was the spokesperson for the entire chain of Pace banks.

"Integrity is our business!"
"We're the friendly place. We care!"

He was on TV, billboards, newspaper ads and flyers. Everyone, but everyone, knew him—John Britton, "the friendly banker."

Mr. Britton's deposition went exactly as I thought it might. They insisted that it be taken in his office and he posed behind a gigantic mahogany desk. He wore a dark-blue single-breasted suit with a matching vest and a watch fob with a gold chain from which a Phi Beta Kappa key was suspended. He glared at me and swore that he came out of his office and saw Mrs. Arnold on the floor. While waiting for the ambulance he comforted her. She told him that she didn't know how the accident happened and that she was sorry for causing any inconvenience.

"In answer to your question, Mr. Ress, we never, ever had any claims or trouble with the entry doors. They always worked perfectly and needless to say there have been no injuries or any history of these doors closing on anyone, ever."

"We are safety-oriented. All accidents are to be reported, but there have been none, not one, except this, since I have been with the bank at this location, which is for the last ten years. These doors are inspected and maintained by a door-safety company and there are no reports of any malfunction whatsoever since I have been with the bank. There is a safety certificate in the file."

It's always a good idea to go over the checkbook. The judge couldn't prohibit it, but he could lay down restrictions. I was allowed to view, but not copy the checks providing I went to the defense attorney's office at a time to be selected by them and did so under their supervision. OK, they set three in the afternoon on a Friday. I was kept waiting in the reception room for half an hour and then escorted into a file room with one table and one chair. No windows. On the table were two big red folders. The secretary said in a very clipped manner:

"You go in there and don't bother anyone. When you're done come out and leave the file. No copies of any checks."

The first thing I noticed is that only one large folder

contained checks. The other was a research file. I opened the door and walked to the secretary's desk. She said:

"I thought I told you not to come out until you're done."

"I think that you gave me a wrong file that shouldn't be there."

"Don't you hear? Don't tell me what we've done. Just go back and finish and leave before five. That's all."

I wanted to go through the checks since it would be my only opportunity. These were the operating records. About fifteen minutes into my review of electric bills, purchases of cleaning materials and office supplies was a check to "Sylvester Door Company" for five hundred and sixty two dollars marked for door repairs. The address was plainly shown and I copied it. Then I found another check to the same company for six hundred and twenty dollars only a month earlier.

Then I looked into the second red folder. There were communications with the insurance company, some from Mr. Britton himself, discussing the bank's exposure for liability in this case, admitting that Mrs. Arnold had been injured by the automatic doors closing on her. The insurance company responded and threatened to withdraw coverage and cancel the policy because of the number of claims caused by the defective front doors closing on people and the bank's failure to repair the doors. Each of the five cases had been settled with a confidentiality provision. The bank's insurance attorney thought that our case could be won if …"we all stand together."

"The witnesses must be properly rewarded for their loyalty." WOW!

A young secretary was walking past the door.

"Excuse me, miss, could you be kind enough to make copies of this for me?"

"Sure."

I had it!

As I was leaving I dropped in on the charming secretary who had seated me.

"I want you to know, again, that you left me private files."

"Just get out of here."

On Saturday I visited the Sylvester Door Company with no subpoena and wearing jeans and a T-shirt.

"Mr. Varner, tell me about the automatic entry doors at the Pace bank."

"Boy, am I glad you came. I have been telling those idiots for over a year now that those doors must be totally replaced. That jerk Britton won't spend the money. I keep fixing them and they keep breaking down and crushing people. We even refer to them as the 'Guillotine Doors'."

I made copies of the repair bills going back over a year along with a great signed statement from Mr. Varner repeating his reference to the "Guillotine Doors."

On Monday I was able to reach the senior partner of the Nazi law firm. He gave me ten minutes of his time which went on for about two hours. After a few phone calls the Arnold case was settled for one hundred and fifty thousand dollars, and at their request I agreed not to file criminal charges against John Britton and his gang of liars and thieves. I don't think that the associate who wanted the employees to "stand together" still works there.

Mrs. Arnold died six months later and her children got the money.

31

You Never Know

Don Fowler was a second-tier partner in our small, crazy, but very successful law firm. He was a good trial lawyer and was handling some of the Aetna's files for us. He started out with the simpler matters, such as suing for damaged property where the Aetna paid out to its policyholder and then Aetna had the right to stand in his or her shoes and sue the person responsible for causing the damage in the first place. It's called "subrogation." Sometimes the biggest problem was getting the Aetna's policyholder, its "assured," to cooperate after they got the insurance money. Don was pretty good at it. We gave Don a buy-out agreement in case he ever left the firm. It compelled us to buy his ownership interest in our firm, which had no market value, for a highly inflated sum. It really was for a sizeable amount, and he had no restrictive clauses about going with another firm, or where he could locate, or taking a client and the files he was working on with him. We prided ourselves on being extra fair.

Don had locked up the subrogation business with the Aetna and started to handle some of their personal injury files. He tried some workers' compensation cases and the Aetna was pleased with him, as were we. We gave him an allowance to entertain the

Aetna adjusters and he was getting files sent to him directly. I was pleased. What I didn't know is that Don had a plan of stealing the Aetna from us and leaving.

One Monday I came into the office and Don's office was empty and all of the Aetna's files were gone! It didn't take long to learn that Don had opened an office in Coral Gables and had not only taken all of the Aetna files, but had one of my attorney friends, Bernie Kessler, call and advise that he was representing Don to make sure that Don received his full payout.

In all fairness I had turned much of the Aetna's work over to Don and didn't protect myself or the firm with a restrictive covenant. My relations with the adjusters at the Aetna had slowly been reduced, in part because Don was handling the client so well.

We still had Travelers, which was another insurance giant. We had been representing Travelers for about two years. It was about two years before when I had received a call from Marty Spencer, the claims manager of the Travelers Insurance Company.

"Lewis, I would like to meet with you and discuss your handling some specialized work for Travelers. I'm only interested in your handling arson cases for us and nothing more."

"Marty, I certainly would be interested."

We met in a small restaurant in Coral Gables. Marty Spencer was a senior claims manager and had been around Miami for over twenty years. He was a bit gruff and very direct.

"Lewis, I know who you are and Bill Connors raves about you. He says that the Aetna has won two huge fire cases as a result of your efforts. You know at the last Claimsmen's

Association meeting no one had heard of anyone ever winning an arson case. The Travelers needs a good arson defense lawyer and if you are interested we would like to retain you, but you understand this will only be for arson cases. That's all. And your firm cannot sue Travelers or its policyholders, so this might not be such a good deal for you."

"Marty, we have considered everything and it would be a feather in our cap to be able to say that we are counsel for the Travelers. We're eager to work with you."

* * * * *

You might wonder what fire cases Bill Connors was talking about. The big arson case involved the destruction by fire of a large clothing manufacturing plant on Miami Beach. The claim was for millions, and if the insurance company doesn't pay they become liable for their assureds' attorneys' fees, which can be astronomical, with interest and costs in addition. Shortly after the extensive fire had occurred I was called in to evaluate the case. One always looks for the point of origin of a fire. Did it come from defective wiring or a water heater or stove or other appliance? There is an entire college dedicated to the study of fires and their causes. Firemen attend, as do insurance experts. I had taken some of their courses. So the first thing I wanted to know is "how did it start?" In this instance the arson was quite clear. The fire was so intense that the sprinkler system went off very shortly. There was a fire trail from the point of origin showing the pattern of how highly flammable liquid was poured over the stored cut clothing. There was little or no doubt that it was arson. The company's books showed the economic problems they were having. The owner had been at the factory earlier on Sunday, the day of the fire.

Clean case? No way. The insurance company had the burden to prove "who done it." It could have been a competitor or a disgruntled employee or an enemy of the owner. We were in luck. There was a five-gallon gasoline can left on the floor. The idiot who started the fire must have figured that it would be consumed in the fire, but no, it was quite intact and it was painted with gray marine type paint. Highly unique and unusual. The fire was caused by someone igniting gasoline. I had an idea. If it had been the owner, he surely would not have wanted to transport a can of gasoline for a long distance.

Let's see if any of the gas stations near the factory saw that can being filled—probably on Sunday, the day of the fire. He would be awfully stupid to fill the can right near the factory, but let's say three or more miles away would be more likely. It took four teams going to service stations in circles radiating out from the factory. Each team had a series of photos, one of which was our factory owner, along with color photos of the gray gas can. Bingo! Exactly five miles from the factory three people picked the owner's photograph as the person having filled the gray painted gas can on Sunday morning, the day of the fire.

The celebration was easing up when I went to the Aetna and asked permission to file criminal charges of arson against their insured, who was suing us for millions. I met with the State's Attorneys' Office and when the story was told they filed a criminal charge on their own. Over the next three years four different prosecutors came and went. Each one had to be briefed by me, prodded, cajoled, begged to go forward. Still no trial. We did all of their work for them. We brought in the witnesses, produced the gray can, showed them the losses on the financial records, photographs of the fire damage, produced experts. Still no trial.

In the meantime I had taken the assured's deposition. He had a good lawyer. The minute I came near the cause of the fire or his client's whereabouts on the day of the fire, he pleaded the Fifth Amendment, refusing to answer on the grounds of possible self-incrimination. The judge delayed the case against the Aetna pending the conclusion of the criminal charges.

Finally the criminal case came up for trial. I was amazed that the defendant, our insured, pleaded "guilty." They withdrew the lawsuit against the Aetna "with prejudice." He plea-bargained and got a year in jail.

* * * * *

That was case number one. Arson case number two was even wilder. There was no doubt that this home fire was caused by an electric wire going from a two hundred and twenty volt room wall air conditioner to a wall outlet. The Aetna insured the developer, "Happy Homes." The tract home was part of a three-hundred-home development. "Life is better in a Happy Home." That was the ad and it worked. Bill Humble had sold out.

The fire occurred in a three-bedroom two-bath house occupied by an African-American family. During the night a blaze started in the living room and the house literally went up in flames. The two daughters had been asleep in the back bedroom and in an effort to get out of the fire they were severely burned all over, badly scarring both sides of their faces, both arms and their backs. They were very nice, sweet, refined young ladies.

One was ten and the other twelve years old. They were innocent victims of a terrible fire.

The fire investigators are generally quite thorough. They narrowed the point of origin of the fire to the electric cord running from the two-ton room wall air conditioner into the wall electric socket. The Sylvan family had asked a neighbor to install the air conditioner, which they had purchased from Sears. They paid him fifty dollars to do the job. He cut through the wall and patched it and plugged it in. The air conditioner had worked just fine for the two weeks that it had been in service. The lawsuit against Bill Humble and Happy Homes was based on a claim that the house was not wired correctly and as a result there was an electric surge which caused the wire connecting the air conditioner to the socket to overheat and actually melt and was the cause of the fire which in turn caused the girls to suffer these horrible permanent injuries. They had a number of electrical experts, including an engineer, ready to testify.

The actual wire had been preserved, and showed that it melted halfway to the plug that fits into the wall socket. The insulation had melted off. The wires were exposed, and copper beads, little balls of metal, showed as a result of the wire itself melting at that point.

I asked to be allowed to have the wire and attached plug examined by our expert. Actually, I didn't have one, but I knew that if it was to be a battle of the experts, after the jury took one good look at those poor mutilated young girls, we would be finished. I could see a possible multi-million dollar verdict. So did the Aetna. I took the electric wire with the melted portion along with the plug to the Dade County Building Department and asked to have their engineer examine it. He was told the story and instructed not to alter the exhibit in any manner. Maybe if there *were* an explanation the jury would be more impressed with the County Building Department Engineer.

Well, I was amazed at what the County Engineer did. He sliced open the plug with a razor, against my instructions, and found out that the plug was for a 220-volt outlet not a 110 outlet, which was the normal wiring of a home. Instead of rewiring the house to accommodate the 220 appliance, the neighbor who installed it had twisted the prong of the plug so that it would fit into a 110 receptacle socket. This was the cause of the surge and the resulting meltdown of the wire and the devastating fire. You had a 220 appliance plugged into a 110 outlet, by virtue of altering the plug.

The County Building Engineer didn't issue a written report and was on standby to testify. We weren't responsible. It was a case to win. What about those poor girls? I'm not a socialist, but it wouldn't be out of place to make some kind of a settlement offer. We did. One hundred thousand dollars.

The plaintiffs' side didn't take the County Engineer's deposition. I was not about to disclose my trump card. They would find some way or phony expert to get around my defense. They never saw it coming. I made the one hundred thousand dollar offer which they rejected out of hand. The case started. It was my turn to make opening statement.

"Ladies and Gentlemen of the jury, how many of you are familiar with Perry Mason? Have you seen his show on TV? Have you seen him in the movies?" They all nodded. Everyone knew of the famous Perry Mason.

"Well, today I am going to be Perry Mason and I am going to solve this mystery right before your eyes and show you how and why this fire started. It will prove without a shred of doubt that my client Happy Homes and Bill Humble were absolutely guiltless and did not in any way cause this terrible fire."

Opposing counsel were dumbstruck. The judge was in a state of shock. No one ever had said anything like that in an opening statement. Either I was crazy or I was "loaded."
Opposing counsel asked for a brief recess.

"Lewis, Are you serious? What in the devil do you have?"

It was Joe Peat and Phil Grey, experienced trial attorneys. They were looking right into my eyes, staring at me.

"Joe, I truly am loaded. If you accept the settlement offer which I am still holding out, but which I am compelled to withdraw once we start the trial itself, I'll show you what I have and you will be satisfied. Bear in mind that I have to live with you both the rest of my professional life."

After a brief conference they said:

"There's no such thing as a bluff here Lewis, We trust you to explain it to us. We'll take the settlement."

We entered into a settlement in open court then I showed them the sliced open plug and explained how the fire happened.

They were pleased to have been offered the opportunity to settle.

*　*　*　*　*

So Don Fowler had taken off with all of our Aetna files. I should have become suspicious when Don Fowler and his wife had failed to show up at a number of office weddings and firm

234

parties, leaving empty seats at the round banquet table. I never thought that he would be this devious. Unfortunately, we were compelled to pay Don Fowler off. I swallowed hard because he took the Aetna, a client that I had nurtured for many years, entertaining the adjusters, taking the supervisors on fishing trips, handling the closing of their homes without charge and visiting the home office in Hartford so many times. Our first major client. Fowler kept the files which were already in our office and which he had the Aetna transfer to him, and he was to handle the Aetna's future work—and to top it off we had to pay him a large sum of money.

We had lost the Aetna, but we had picked up Travelers. During the two years that we had been representing Travelers we had developed close ties with them and they were now sending us their full line of cases to defend. We did everything for the Travelers that we had done for the Aetna.

Then one day the phone rang.

"Lewis, Marty Spencer talking."

"Yes, Marty."

"Lewis, Travelers has bought out Aetna's casualty business. Aetna is just going to handle group medical insurance. I have had all of the Aetna's files picked up from Don Fowler and they are in a truck on its way to your office right now. You've worked on some of these files already. I will be adding a number of relatively new Aetna files. I hope you and your firm continue to represent us as well as you have been doing."

"Marty, thanks. Thanks a million!"

Made in the USA
Monee, IL
06 February 2022